Contents

Answers to Revision Questions are online at:
www.hodderplus.co.uk/cceagcsescience

Introduction

Using this revision book will help you fulfil your potential in the CCEA GCSE Science: Single Award course. The chapters follow both the order of the specification and the chapter order in the textbook for the CCEA GCSE Science: Single Award course.

This revision book has been written in a readable and easily understood style with numerous sub-headings and short sections that clearly explain the key points. It contains only the important content – everything that is included is important!

As well as helping with knowledge and understanding, this book contains useful guidance in examination technique in the form of **Exam tips**. Exam tips are interspersed throughout the text and provide valuable tips that will help each student maximise examination performance.

Worked examples are included in each chapter. These give model answers to exam-type questions. At the end of each chapter, **Revision questions** are present to reinforce knowledge and understanding of key points. Most of the revision questions are written in a style similar to how the topics are typically asked in examinations. Answers to these revision questions are provided on the website www.hodderplus.co.uk/cceagcsescience

A separate **Glossary** is included for each of the different sciences (Units). Each glossary explains the key terms that students should know and understand in each examination.

Higher-tier content only is colour coded in pink to make it easy for students to identify what they need to know.

Using a carefully planned revision strategy which incorporates the reinforcement of core knowledge and essential understanding, this book will enable you to achieve your very best, whether that is striving to obtain an A or A* grade or whether it is hoping to achieve a grade C.

Helpful hints

This book will help you learn and understand key content and concepts – the key requirement in taking an examination. However, it is important to understand that many students also lose marks through not answering the question exactly as it is asked or by not providing sufficient detail – i.e. through poor examination technique.

The words in the table at the top of the next page are often used in examination papers and it is important that you understand exactly what each of them means. These words are often called 'command' words – they tell you what to do in each question.

If you are asked to 'Use the graph/table/information given **and** your knowledge' some of the answer will be provided in the data – some will not. If you are asked to 'Use **only** the information given' then all of the information needed for the answer is provided in the data.

'Command' word	What you need to do
Name/Give/State	Write down a short answer – possibly only one word – no explanation is needed
Complete	Answer in spaces that have been provided – sometimes in boxes on diagrams or in tables or on answer lines at the end of questions or in the gaps within a written paragraph
Describe	Give a detailed account
Explain	Include an explanation of why or how
Compare	Describe the similarities and/or differences in the information
Suggest/Predict	Although you will not be expected to know the answer, you should be able to deduce or estimate it, either from information provided or from scientific knowledge
Calculate	Work out the answer (usually involving a mathematical process)
Circle	Draw a circle around the correct answer. The correct answer will be given (together with some incorrect answers)
Choose from	The correct answer must be selected from those given – the alternatives are usually given in a list in bold

The number of marks available for a question part gives a clue about how much detail is usually required. For example, a three-mark question usually requires three specific points. The wording of the question itself often gives a clue. For example, 'Describe fully' requires more information that 'Describe'.

In Foundation-Tier papers there will be one extended prose Quality of Written Communication (QWC) six-mark question and there will be two of these on each Higher-Tier paper. Remember, that while good written English is important, most of the marks in these questions are for correct science. It is important that these questions are read carefully to work out exactly what is required.

You should remember that each examination paper will test a wide range of skills (as well as knowledge and understanding). Skills tested include the interpretation of short passages of text, diagrams, graphs and tables, and the drawing of graphs, performing calculations and writing formulae or equations.

Other useful sources

Past papers are a very useful source of information. Past papers can be found on the CCEA website (www.ccea.org.uk). These will show how questions are often asked in particular topics. **Mark schemes** for past papers are also available. These are also very important as they provide information as to what answers are acceptable for particular questions. **Chief Examiner's Reports** (also on the CCEA website) provide feedback on how candidates performed in each examination in each series. They are very useful as they explain the common mistakes that students often make in particular questions. The CCEA website also contains the Science: Single Award **specification** (course). The specification outlines the course and tells teachers and students exactly what is required to be studied in each topic.

1 Food and energy

Food types

Revised

We need a number of different **types** of food to keep us healthy. Food is also a source of **chemical energy**.

The following table shows the main food types we need.

Food type	Needed in body for	Examples
carbohydrate (starch)	energy (slow-release)	potato, bread
carbohydrate (sugar)	energy (fast-release)	cake, biscuits
protein	growth and repair	fish, beans
fat	energy store	sausages, butter
vitamin C	healthy teeth and gums	oranges, lemons
vitamin D	strong bones and teeth	fish, milk
calcium (mineral)	strong bones and teeth	milk, cheese
iron (mineral)	helping blood to carry oxygen	red meat, spinach
water	a solvent and medium for chemical reactions	
fibre	preventing constipation and helping protect against bowel cancer	wholemeal bread, green vegetables

Food tests

Revised

Food tests can be used to identify the food types present in different kinds of food.

Food type	Test	Method	Result (if food type present)
starch	starch test	add iodine solution	iodine turns from yellow-brown to blue-black
sugar	Benedict's test	add Benedict's solution and heat in a water bath	the solution changes from blue to a brick-red colour
protein	biuret test	add sodium hydroxide, then a few drops of copper sulfate and shake	the solution turns from a blue colour to a purple, mauve or lilac colour
fat	emulsion test	shake the fat with alcohol, then add an equal amount of water	a cloudy white substance is formed

> **Exam tip**
>
> Most foods contain more than one food type – e.g. bacon contains protein, fat and water.

Respiration

Revised

Respiration is how we use carbohydrate (and sometimes fat) to provide **energy**.

The word equation for respiration is:

glucose + oxygen → carbon dioxide + water + energy

Comparing the energy content in different foods

The apparatus shown in Figure 1.1 can be used to **compare** the energy in different foods.

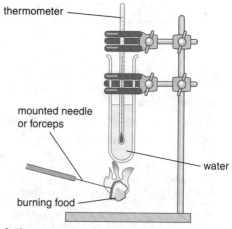

↑ Figure 1.1 Measuring the energy content of food

thermometer

mounted needle or forceps

water

burning food

To make sure results are valid (a fair test) when comparing different foods:
- use the same amount of each food
- hold the burning food the same distance from the boiling tube
- use the same amount of water.

Some (heat) energy will be:
- lost to the air
- lost to heat the glass
- left in the burnt food remains.

↑ Figure 1.2 Key things you must know in food-burning investigations

Exam tip

Many exam questions ask about **validity** and why all the energy in a food is not used to heat the water (i.e. why some is **lost**).

How much energy do we need?

Different people need different amounts of energy.

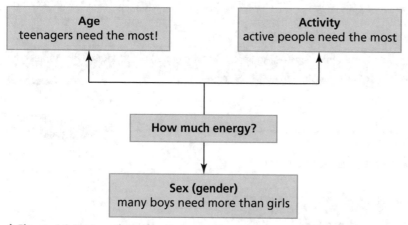

Age
teenagers need the most!

Activity
active people need the most

How much energy?

Sex (gender)
many boys need more than girls

↑ Figure 1.3 Factors that affect our energy needs

Exam tip

These factors are often interlinked and not always true – e.g. some girls need more energy than some boys because they are more active.

Diet and health  Revised

There is a clear link between diet and health.

Circulatory diseases

The link between diet and health is very obvious with **circulatory diseases** – diseases that affect the heart and/or blood vessels.

Heart disease is an example.

Heart disease can cause a **heart attack**:

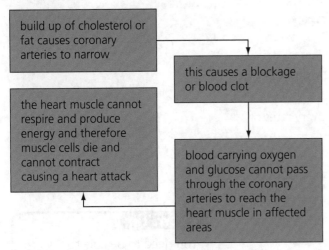

↑ **Figure 1.4 How heart attacks happen**

There are many factors that can contribute to heart disease.

Therefore there are many things we can do to reduce our chances of getting heart disease – these can be grouped into **lifestyle** and **diet factors** as shown in Figure 1.5.

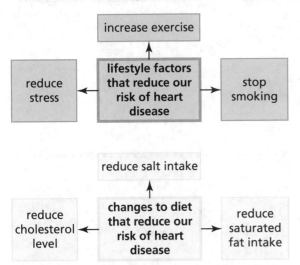

↑ **Figure 1.5 Lifestyle and diet factors that can help to reduce heart disease**

Strokes are also examples of circulatory diseases, but they affect the **brain** – the factors listed above that help in protecting against heart disease also help in protecting against strokes.

However, many people fail to change their diet or lifestyle and remain at risk of heart attack or stroke.

Exam tip

You need to know the difference between lifestyle and diet factors.

The costs of circulatory diseases

Circulatory diseases are expensive to treat because:

● many patients are ill (in hospital) for a **long time**

● **expensive drugs** and **medicines** are often needed

● many **highly-trained staff** are needed.

Families are affected because a parent may not be able to work or requires a lot of care if the parent has a circulatory disease.

The effect of exercise on heart rate and recovery rate

You can help your heart and protect against heart disease by doing exercise.

Figure 1.6 shows the effect of exercise on the heart and recovery rates of two girls.

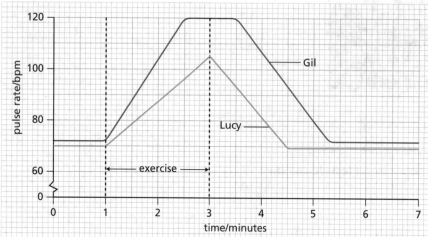

↑ Figure 1.6 The effect of exercise on heart rate

> **Exam tip**
>
> You need to be able to interpret graphs like these – e.g. understanding when exercise starts, working out increases in heart rate and comparing recovery times.

Recovery time is the length of time it takes after exercise for the pulse/heart rate to return to normal (the resting rate).

Worked example

From the graph state:

a) When exercise started.

b) The maximum increase in pulse rate for Lucy.

c) The maximum percentage pulse rate increase for Lucy.

d) Lucy's recovery time.

e) Two things that suggest that Gil is less fit than Lucy.

Answer

a) 1 minute

b) $105 - 70 = 35$

c) $\frac{35}{70} \times 100 = 50\%$

d) 3 min to 4.5 min = 1.5 minutes

e) Any two from: Gil's resting rate is higher / her rate increases more during exercise / her recovery time is longer

Regular exercise also helps strengthen the heart muscle. This increases the amount of blood pumped in each beat, even when at rest. This allows the heart to pump less often (pumping the same amount of blood) and, therefore, the heart suffers less wear and tear.

> **Exam tip**
>
> Regular exercise can also help in preventing obesity – obesity puts a lot of strain on the heart (because the heart has to supply a much bigger body).

Other health problems associated with food

- **Anorexia:** eating less than required to maintain weight – most common in young females.
- **Bulimia:** binge eating followed by induced vomiting – also leads to weight loss.

Photosynthesis

This is how plants make food using light energy. The word equation for photosynthesis is:

carbon dioxide + water → glucose + oxygen

The glucose produced during photosynthesis is usually converted into starch for storage. One way of showing that photosynthesis has taken place is by showing that **starch** is present in a leaf.

This can be done using a **starch test** as described in the following table.

Step	Method	Reason
1	put the leaf in boiling water	kills the leaf and stops further reactions
2	boil the leaf in alcohol (this must be done in a water bath because alcohol is flammable)	removes chlorophyll (green colour) from the leaf
3	dip the leaf in boiling water again	makes the leaf soft and less brittle (boiling in alcohol makes a leaf rigid)
4	spread the leaf on a white tile and add iodine	if starch present the iodine will turn from yellow-brown to blue-black

Showing that light is needed for photosynthesis

- Partially cover a leaf on a plant with foil.
- Put the plant in bright light for at least 24 hours.
- Test the leaf for starch.

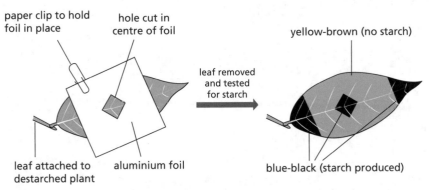

paper clip to hold foil in place
hole cut in centre of foil
yellow-brown (no starch)
leaf removed and tested for starch
leaf attached to destarched plant
aluminium foil
blue-black (starch produced)

↑ **Figure 1.7 Light is needed for photosynthesis**

Figure 1.7 shows that starch is only produced in those parts of the leaf that receive light. The conclusion is that light is needed for photosynthesis.

Before carrying out the above experiment it is important to destarch the plant. This involves leaving it in the dark for 48 hours. This ensures that there is no starch left in the leaves at the start of the experiment.

Palisade cells

Palisade cells are specialised cells found in a layer near the top of leaves.

They are highly adapted for photosynthesis as shown in Figure 1.8.

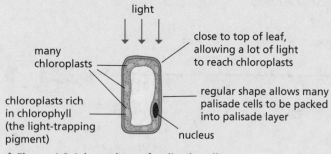

↑ Figure 1.8 Adaptations of palisade cells

Exam tip

Figure 1.8 describes four ways in which palisade cells are adapted. Questions about palisade cells are almost always about these adaptations.

Food chains and food webs (the interdependence of living organisms)

Revised

A **food chain** describes the order in which energy passes through living organisms – i.e. a feeding sequence.

The **Sun** is the initial **source of energy** for all food chains.

A food chain always follows the order:

producer → primary consumer → secondary consumer → tertiary consumer

Exam tip

The **arrows** in a food chain show the direction of **energy flow**.

	Producer	Primary consumer	Secondary consumer	Tertiary consumer
Description	a plant that makes food by photosynthesis	an animal that feeds on a plant	an animal that feeds on a primary consumer	an animal that feeds on a secondary consumer
Example	grass	leaf-eating insect	beetle	insect-eating bird

Exam tip

Animals need plants both as an initial **food source** and also to provide **oxygen** through photosynthesis.

Food webs show how a number of food chains are interlinked. They are more realistic because very few consumers feed on only one thing.

1 Describe the food test for sugar. Describe the colour change you would expect if sugar is present. **[3 marks]**

2 Apart from energy, name two other products of respiration. **[2 marks]**

3 Have another look at Figure 1.7 – the results of the investigation showing that light is needed for photosynthesis. Suggest what would have happened if the leaf had not been destarched at the start of the investigation. **[2 marks]**

4 The apparatus below can be used to measure the rate of photosynthesis under different conditions.

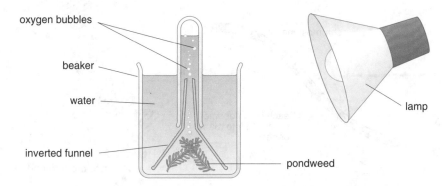

Suggest how you could use this apparatus to investigate the effect of light intensity on rate of photosynthesis. **[3 marks]**

5 The diagram below shows a grassland food web.

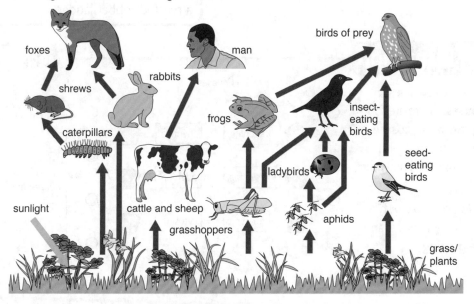

a) What is the original source of energy for a food web? [1]

b) Draw a food chain involving three different organisms. [2]

c) How many food chains are there that involve four different organisms. [1]

d) Suggest what would happen to the number of grasshoppers if the number of birds of prey decreased. Explain your answer. [2]   **[6 marks]**

Go online for the answers

Online

2 Chromosomes and genes

Living organisms are made up of small units called **cells**. Most cells contain a **nucleus**, the control centre of the cell.

Chromosomes, genes and DNA

Revised

The nucleus contains **chromosomes** and these control development.

Figure 2.1 shows that a chromosome is divided into many **genes**.

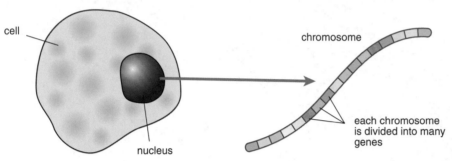

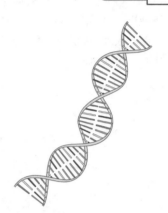

↑ Figure 2.1 Chromosomes and genes

↑ Figure 2.2 A section of the DNA double helix

Each gene controls a particular characteristic (feature) – such as eye colour.

Chromosomes are made up of the chemical **DNA** which is formed into a **double helix** shape.

Exam tip

Think of the structure of DNA as a twisted rubber ladder.

DNA and protein formation

Revised

DNA consists of two strands (or backbones) joined together by pairs of **bases**. There are four types of bases – **adenine**, **guanine**, **cytosine** and **thymine**. Only adenine (A) can link with thymine (T), and only cytosine (C) can link with guanine (G).

Figure 2.3 shows a small section of DNA with only A–T (or T–A), or C–G (or G–C) links – an arrangement known as **base pairing**.

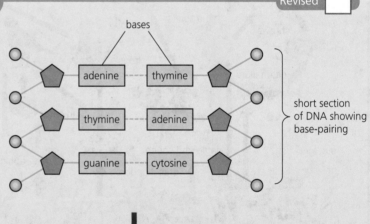

short section of DNA showing base-pairing

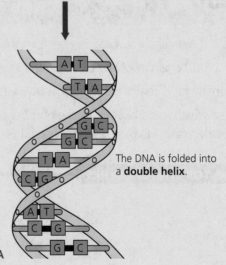

The DNA is folded into a **double helix**.

→ Figure 2.3 The structure of DNA

The role of DNA

The bases along one side (the coding strand) of the DNA provide the code for the cell to make **amino acids** (building blocks of protein), which in turn are linked together to form **proteins**. Proteins are very important molecules – they control how a cell functions and develops.

This process of protein building (protein synthesis) is summarised in Figure 2.4.

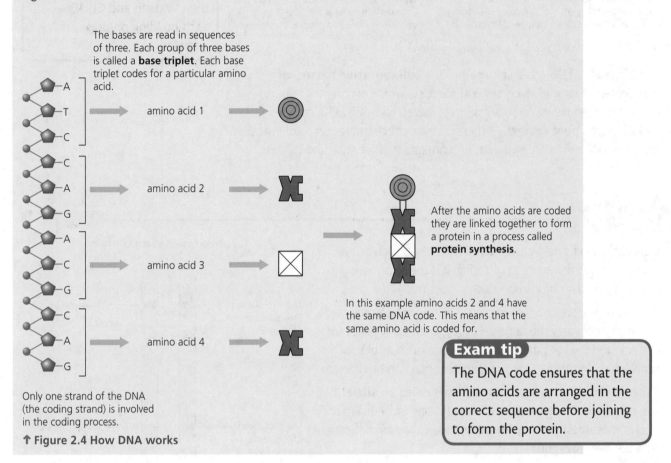

The bases are read in sequences of three. Each group of three bases is called a **base triplet**. Each base triplet codes for a particular amino acid.

After the amino acids are coded they are linked together to form a protein in a process called **protein synthesis**.

In this example amino acids 2 and 4 have the same DNA code. This means that the same amino acid is coded for.

Only one strand of the DNA (the coding strand) is involved in the coding process.

↑ **Figure 2.4 How DNA works**

Exam tip

The DNA code ensures that the amino acids are arranged in the correct sequence before joining to form the protein.

Worked example

a) A length of DNA consists of 180 bases. How many amino acids does this section code for? Explain your answer.

b) In the same section, 60 of the bases are thymine. How many guanine bases are there in the section?

Answer

a) 30; only half the bases are in the coding strand. In the coding strand (90 bases) each sequence of three bases (base triplet) produces one amino acid.

b) If 60 bases are thymine then 60 bases are adenine because A and T always code together (total 120). The remaining 60 must be 30 guanine and 30 cytosine because C and G always code together.

Building the theory – working out the structure of DNA

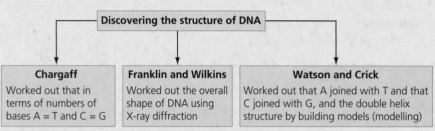

Chargaff	Franklin and Wilkins	Watson and Crick
Worked out that in terms of numbers of bases A = T and C = G	Worked out the overall shape of DNA using X-ray diffraction	Worked out that A joined with T and that C joined with G, and the double helix structure by building models (modelling)

Discovering the structure of DNA

⬆ Figure 2.5 Working out the structure of DNA

The discovery of DNA is an example of the **collaborative nature of science** – the way in which **several** scientists work together to make new discoveries by building up information in stages. New scientific knowledge is validated by **peer review** – other scientists check the research to ensure that new discoveries are based on experiments that are valid and reliable.

Exam tip

You should know that Chargaff's work came first, then Franklin and Wilkins', then Watson and Crick's – each building on previous knowledge.

Genetics

Revised

Genetics explains how characteristics (features) such as eye colour pass from parents to offspring. It is the information in the genes on the chromosomes that does this.

Chromosomes are arranged in pairs – in any one pair the two chromosomes carry the same genes (e.g. both carry genes for eye colour). However, the form of the gene (such as blue or brown eyes) in the two partner chromosomes can be different.

If a gene exists in two forms, each form is called an **allele**. If the two alleles of a gene are the same (in one individual/pair of chromosomes) they are **homozygous**; if they are different they are **heterozygous**.

Sexual and asexual reproduction

Understanding genetics requires an understanding of sexual reproduction.

Sexual reproduction occurs when gametes (sex cells) from male and female parents combine to form a new individual. **Gametes** have half the number of chromosomes (i.e. one from each pair) that other body cells have.

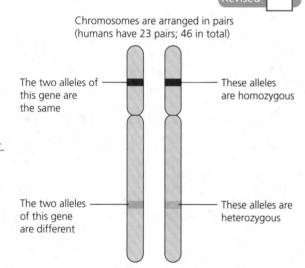

Chromosomes are arranged in pairs (humans have 23 pairs; 46 in total)

The two alleles of this gene are the same

These alleles are homozygous

The two alleles of this gene are different

These alleles are heterozygous

⬆ Figure 2.6 Chromosomes, genes and alleles

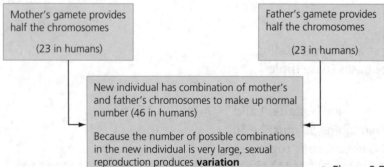

Mother's gamete provides half the chromosomes

(23 in humans)

Father's gamete provides half the chromosomes

(23 in humans)

New individual has combination of mother's and father's chromosomes to make up normal number (46 in humans)

Because the number of possible combinations in the new individual is very large, sexual reproduction produces **variation**

⬅ Figure 2.7 Sexual reproduction and variation

In **asexual reproduction** only one parent is involved and the offspring are **genetically identical (clones)** of the parent.

Genetic diagrams

Genetics questions in *Science: Single Award* cover only the variation produced by one gene and its pair of alleles.

Some key features about genetic crosses:

- the crosses are always about **one characteristic** – e.g. eye colour, flower colour, height in peas
- **phenotype** – this is the outward appearance of an individual or feature; e.g. blue eyes
- **genotype** – this is a set of paired symbols, representing the two alleles in an individual
- **dominant allele** – in a heterozygous individual, the dominant allele overrides the non-dominant recessive allele
- **recessive allele** – the recessive allele is dominated by the dominant allele; the recessive feature only shows itself in the phenotype if there are two recessive alleles (and no dominant allele)
- when setting out a genetic cross it is usually in the sequence parents phenotypes; parents genotypes; gametes; offspring; offspring genotypes; offspring phenotypes as shown in Figure 2.8.

Typical example of a genetic cross

In pea plants, seeds are either round or wrinkled. Seed shape is controlled by one gene (on each of two partner chromosomes) but there can be two different alleles. The allele for round seed is dominant to the (recessive) allele for wrinkled seed – the alleles are given the symbols R (for round) and r (for wrinkled).

Figure 2.8 shows the offspring genotypes and phenotypes produced from a cross between two pea plants, each heterozygous for seed shape.

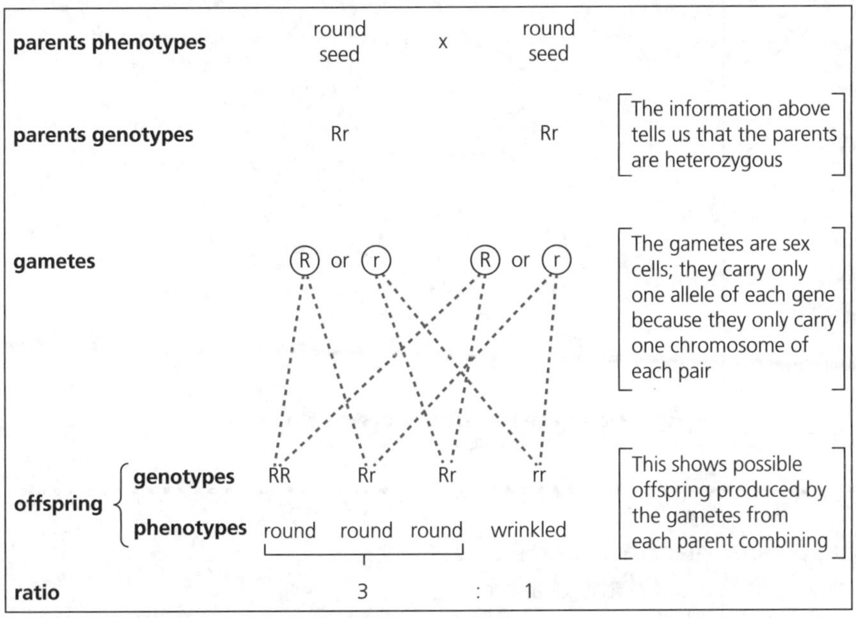

> **Exam tip**
>
> The gametes produced by one parent can combine only with the gametes in another parent – the different gametes of the same individual cannot combine.

> **Exam tip**
>
> You only get two different types of gametes in one individual if it is heterozygous.

> **Exam tip**
>
> Ratios are accurate only when large numbers of offspring are involved. For example, if there were only two seeds produced in the cross opposite, it cannot be 3:1.

parents phenotypes	round seed	x	round seed	
parents genotypes	Rr		Rr	The information above tells us that the parents are heterozygous
gametes	ⓇorⓇ		ⓇorⓇ	The gametes are sex cells; they carry only one allele of each gene because they only carry one chromosome of each pair
offspring genotypes	RR Rr Rr rr			This shows possible offspring produced by the gametes from each parent combining
offspring phenotypes	round round round wrinkled			
ratio	3 : 1			

↑ **Figure 2.8 A genetic cross showing how two heterozygous parents produce offspring in a 3:1 ratio**

Figure 2.9 shows how a Punnett square can be used. In this example, using seed shape in peas as before, a heterozygote (Rr) is crossed with a homozygous recessive (rr) pea.

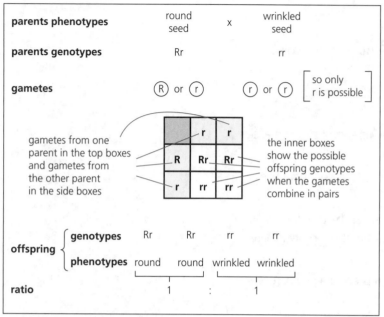

↑ Figure 2.9 Using a Punnett square

Exam tip

It is usually easier to work crosses out using **Punnett squares**.

Exam tip

If the offspring ratio is 3:1 in a genetic cross, then both parents must have been **heterozygous**.

Exam tip

If the offspring ratio is 1:1, then one parent is **heterozygous** and the other is **homozygous recessive**.

Worked example

Brown eyes are dominant to blue eyes. Using the symbols B for brown and b for blue, use a Punnett square show how brown-eyed parents can have children with blue eyes.

Answer

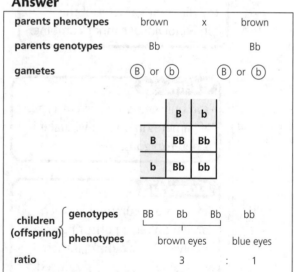

← Figure 2.10 The genetics of eye colour

Higher tier candidates must be able to interpret pedigree diagrams – see the pedigree diagram in the Revision questions at the end of this chapter.

Inherited diseases

Some medical conditions – such as cystic fibrosis – can be inherited. **Inherited conditions** are passed on **genetically** (in DNA) from parent to child.

Cystic fibrosis is caused by having two recessive alleles of a particular gene. Individuals who do not possess this recessive allele (homozygous dominant) or who are heterozygous (only one copy) do not have the condition.

An individual with cystic fibrosis is usually produced by parents who are heterozygous (carriers) for this gene, as shown in Fig 2.11.

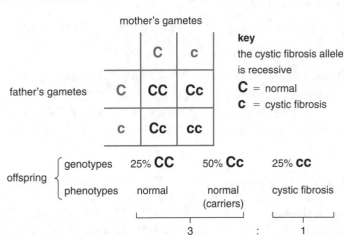

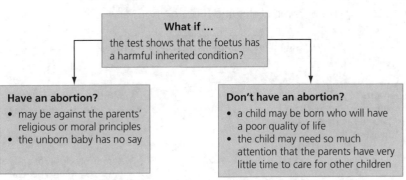

↑ **Figure 2.11 The inheritance of cystic fibrosis**

Inherited disease and ethical issues

It is possible to test for some inherited conditions by carrying out tests on the foetus when it is in the uterus (womb). However, taking such a test can raise ethical issues.

What if …
the test shows that the foetus has a harmful inherited condition?

Have an abortion?
- may be against the parents' religious or moral principles
- the unborn baby has no say

Don't have an abortion?
- a child may be born who will have a poor quality of life
- the child may need so much attention that the parents have very little time to care for other children

↑ **Figure 2.12 The ethics of testing for foetal abnormalities**

Genetic screening

Revised

Genetic screening means testing for genetic conditions – the foetus can be screened, but for some conditions the parents can be tested before becoming pregnant. The screening checks if the parents have alleles that could result in a child with an inherited condition.

Down syndrome is a human condition caused by having an extra chromosome (47 rather than 46). For many years it has been possible to test a foetus to check if it will develop Down syndrome.

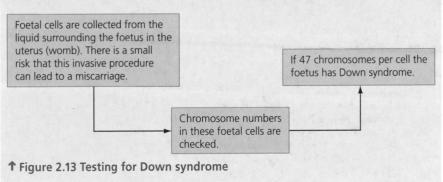

Foetal cells are collected from the liquid surrounding the foetus in the uterus (womb). There is a small risk that this invasive procedure can lead to a miscarriage.

If 47 chromosomes per cell the foetus has Down syndrome.

Chromosome numbers in these foetal cells are checked.

↑ **Figure 2.13 Testing for Down syndrome**

Exam tip

Because of the risk of miscarriage when testing for Down syndrome, the test is usually recommended only for older mothers where the risk of Down syndrome is higher.

There are many wider **ethical issues** associated with screening for genetic conditions:

● should you be allowed a free choice whether to screen or not?
● should you be allowed to screen for the sex of the child?
● should cost be a factor?
● who should be allowed access to the information – should it be available to insurance companies and employers? If insurance companies have genetic information that someone is more likely to die young, will insurance be more difficult to get and will it be more expensive?

Gene therapy

Gene therapy can be used to treat some inherited diseases. The process involves replacing the 'faulty' gene (allele) with a normal-functioning gene. For cystic fibrosis this involves spraying the 'normal' alleles into the lungs – a part of the body badly affected by cystic fibrosis. Some of the cells in the lung take up the sprayed alleles and function normally.

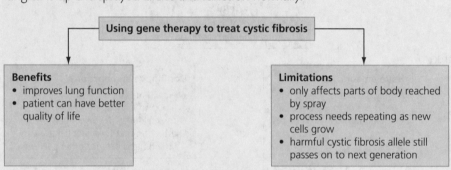

Using gene therapy to treat cystic fibrosis

Benefits
• improves lung function
• patient can have better quality of life

Limitations
• only affects parts of body reached by spray
• process needs repeating as new cells grow
• harmful cystic fibrosis allele still passes on to next generation

← Figure 2.14 Using gene therapy to treat cystic fibrosis

Genetic engineering – genetically modified (GM) crops

Revised

Genetic engineering is the transfer of DNA (genes) from one type of organism (species) to another.

In GM crops this involves transferring DNA into a crop to give it qualities it wouldn't otherwise have. For example, DNA from bacteria is incorporated into maize to give it pest-resistant properties – insect pests are unable to feed on it.

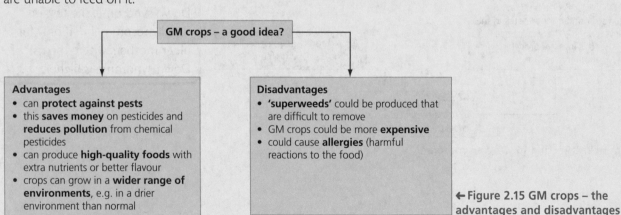

GM crops – a good idea?

Advantages
• can **protect against pests**
• this **saves money** on pesticides and **reduces pollution** from chemical pesticides
• can produce **high-quality foods** with extra nutrients or better flavour
• crops can grow in a **wider range of environments**, e.g. in a drier environment than normal

Disadvantages
• 'superweeds' could be produced that are difficult to remove
• GM crops could be more **expensive**
• could cause **allergies** (harmful reactions to the food)

← Figure 2.15 GM crops – the advantages and disadvantages

Most scientists argue that the advantages of GM crops outweigh the disadvantages.

1 Put the following structures in order of size starting with the smallest:

chromosome   cell   nucleus   gene   base   [1 mark]

2 The following table shows the percentage of different bases in the DNA of two different organisms.

Organism	Adenine	Guanine	Cytosine	Thymine
A	20%	30%		
B			14%	

a) Copy and complete the table. [3]

b) Explain how DNA codes for protein. [3]   **[6 marks]**

3 Explain the difference between the terms homozygous and heterozygous.   **[2 marks]**

4 Pea plants can be either tall or short. When two tall plants were crossed three quarters of the offspring were tall and the rest short.

a) Copy and complete the genetic diagram below to explain the outcome of this cross. [2]

		t
	Tt	

b) Copy and complete the offspring genotypes for the cross above.

Genotypes _____ : Tt : _____ : _____ [1]

Phenotypes _____ : tall : _____ : _____ [1]   **[4 marks]**

5 Huntington's disease is a rare medical condition caused by the presence of a single allele. The pedigree diagram shows the inheritance of Huntington's disease in a family through three generations.

a) How many female grandchildren do individuals 1 and 2 have? [1]

b) What is the evidence that the allele for Huntington's disease is dominant and not recessive? [1]

c) Explain the pattern of transmission of Huntington's disease between the parents (1 and 2) and their children. [3]   **[5 marks]**

Key

☐ Normal male

○ Normal female

■ Male with Huntington's disease

● Female with Huntington's disease

6 a) Explain the term 'genetic screening'. [1]

b) Give one example of a medical condition that can be identified by genetic screening. [1]   **[2 marks]**

7 a) Explain the term 'GM crop'. [2]

b) Give two arguments for growing GM crops. [2]   **[4 marks]**

3 Nervous system and hormones

Both the nervous system and hormones are involved in sensing and responding to changes (stimuli) in the environment.

The nervous system

Revised

The role of the nervous system is shown in Figure 3.1. The arrows represent **neurones** (nerve cells) that carry **nerve impulses** (electrical charges) between the different sections.

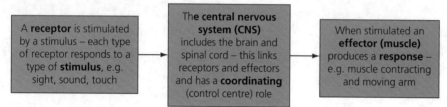

| A **receptor** is stimulated by a stimulus – each type of receptor responds to a type of **stimulus**, e.g. sight, sound, touch | → | The **central nervous system (CNS)** includes the brain and spinal cord – this links receptors and effectors and has a **coordinating** (control centre) role | → | When stimulated an **effector (muscle)** produces a **response** – e.g. muscle contracting and moving arm |

↑ **Figure 3.1 The nervous system**

Voluntary and reflex actions

Voluntary and **reflex** actions are the two main types of nervous actions as summarised in the table below.

	Voluntary	Reflex
Thinking time (brain) involved	yes	no
Speed of action	variable – usually much slower	fast

> **Exam tip**
> Reflexes are **automatic** and often **protective** – such as the withdrawal of a hand from a hot object.

Hormones

Revised

Hormones are **chemical messengers** that travel in the **blood** to bring about a response in a **target organ.**

The main differences between the nervous system and hormones are summarised in the table below.

	Nervous system	Hormones
Method of communication	impulses along neurones	chemicals in blood
Speed of action	fast-acting	usually slow-acting

Sensitivity (hormones) in plants

Plants also respond to environmental change. **Phototropism** is the growth response involving plants bending in the direction of light. This response is controlled by a **hormone** called auxin.

Phototropism works like this:

- auxin (hormone) produced in tip moves to shaded side of the plant
- auxin causes more growth on the shaded side
- the plant bends towards the light – because there is more growth on the shaded side than the illuminated side.

> **Exam tip**
> By bending in the direction of the light, the plant gets **more light** and so **more photosynthesis** and more **growth** happens on that side.

The male and female reproductive systems

Mammals, including humans, produce young by **sexual reproduction**. This involves the joining together (fusion) of two **gametes** (sex cells) – the sperm and the egg (ovum).

The **male reproductive system** makes sperm and helps the sperm to enter the female.

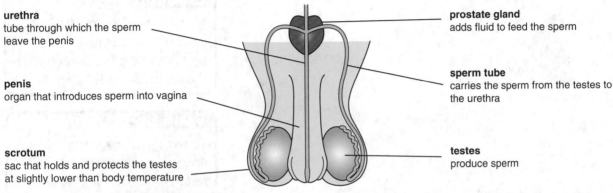

urethra
tube through which the sperm leave the penis

penis
organ that introduces sperm into vagina

scrotum
sac that holds and protects the testes at slightly lower than body temperature

prostate gland
adds fluid to feed the sperm

sperm tube
carries the sperm from the testes to the urethra

testes
produce sperm

↑ **Figure 3.2 The male reproductive system**

The **female reproductive system** is where fertilisation (joining of sperm and egg) takes place and this is also where the foetus (baby) develops.

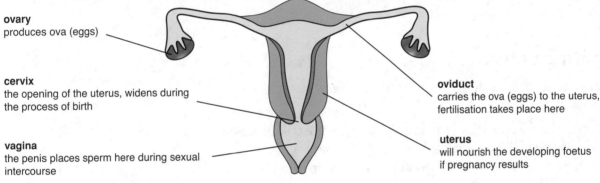

ovary
produces ova (eggs)

cervix
the opening of the uterus, widens during the process of birth

vagina
the penis places sperm here during sexual intercourse

oviduct
carries the ova (eggs) to the uterus, fertilisation takes place here

uterus
will nourish the developing foetus if pregnancy results

↑ **Figure 3.3 The female reproductive system**

Hormones and the menstrual cycle

The process of menstruation (having periods) starts in girls at puberty and continues until the end of a woman's reproductive life. The function of the menstrual cycle is the monthly renewal of the delicate blood-rich lining of the uterus, so that it will provide a suitable environment for the embryo should fertilisation occur.

The **menstrual cycle**:

- lasts (approximately) 28 days
- the ovum is released (**ovulation**) on day 14 (approximately) – by this time the uterine lining has built up in preparation for pregnancy
- sexual reproduction can result in pregnancy if it occurs in a short window on either side of ovulation
- **menstruation** is the breakdown and removal of the blood-rich uterine lining at the end of each cycle.

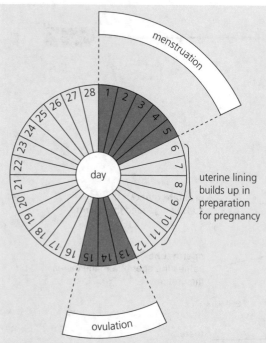

↑ Figure 3.4 The menstrual cycle

Exam tip

The levels of oestrogen and progesterone peak at the time of the cycle when they are most active – oestrogen peaks just before ovulation and progesterone after.

Exam tip

Menstruation occurs when the levels of both oestrogen and progesterone fall at the end of the menstrual cycle.

Exam tip

The menstrual cycle stops if pregnancy occurs and only restarts after the baby is born.

The menstrual cycle is controlled by **hormones** including:

● **oestrogen** – this stimulates ovulation and starts the build-up and repair of the uterine wall

● **progesterone** – this continues the build-up of the uterine lining after ovulation.

Preventing pregnancy

Contraception reduces (or stops) the possibility of pregnancy occurring when having sex.

Some people, who are opposed to contraception, can reduce the chances of pregnancy by avoiding having sex around the time of ovulation each month. This has been called the **rhythm** or **natural method** of contraception.

The three main types of contraception are:

● physical

● chemical

● surgical.

Type	Example	Method	Advantages	Disadvantages
physical	condom	acts as a barrier to prevent sperm entering the female	protects against sexually transmitted diseases – easily obtained and easy to use	unreliable if not used properly or gets damaged
chemical	contraceptive pill	taken by a female to change her hormone levels to prevent ovaries releasing eggs	very reliable	some side-effects, such as weight gain
surgical	vasectomy	cutting sperm tubes, preventing sperm from reaching the penis	virtually 100% reliable	very difficult or impossible to reverse
surgical	female sterilisation	cutting oviducts, preventing ova from reaching the uterus or being fertilised	virtually 100% reliable	very difficult or impossible to reverse

Worked example

Suggest why condoms are a widely used contraceptive for young married couples who have no children.

Answer

Condoms are not permanent (sterilisation is) and they will probably want to have children later.

Condoms have no side-effects, which the contraceptive pill often has. They are also easily obtained.

Insulin

Revised

Insulin is a hormone that reduces blood glucose levels. It is important that the amount of glucose (sugar) in the blood is at just the right level.

Figure 3.5 shows how insulin stops the blood glucose levels from rising too high.

Exam tip

The action of insulin highlights the definition of a hormone discussed earlier.

Insulin is a **chemical** messenger that travels in the **blood** to bring about a response (converting **glucose** to **glycogen**) in the **liver** (target organ).

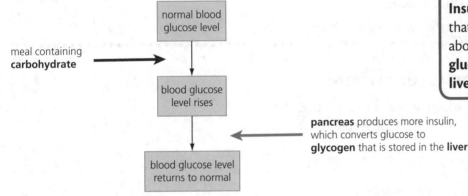

↑ **Figure 3.5 The action of insulin**

Worked example

a) Explain why the body needs glucose in the blood.

b) Suggest why the level of insulin in the blood is usually at its lowest in the middle of the night.

Answer

a) The glucose is transported to body cells to provide energy in respiration.

b) Glucose levels will also be low during the night. By this time the glucose from the last meal of the day has been used up in respiration or converted to glycogen for storage.

Diabetes

Diabetes is a lifelong condition in which the body does not produce enough insulin (or the insulin produced does not work). Therefore, people with diabetes have very high (and dangerous) blood glucose levels unless treated.

The **symptoms** (signs that show something is wrong) of diabetes include:

- glucose (sugar) in the urine
- thirst
- needing to go to the toilet often
- coma – if diagnosis and treatment is delayed too long.

The main differences between the two types of diabetes are summarised in the table below.

	Type 1	Type 2
Main effect	insulin is not produced by the pancreas	insulin is produced but stops working properly
Treatment	insulin injections – plus controlled diet and exercise	usually controlled by diet and exercise
Preventative measures	none – not caused by lifestyle	take exercise, reduce sugar intake, avoid obesity
Age of first occurrence	often in childhood	usually as an adult

Worked example

a) Suggest why people with diabetes are encouraged to exercise more.

b) Suggest why lots of younger people are being diagnosed with Type 2 diabetes.

Answer

a) Exercise uses up glucose in respiration and therefore avoids (damaging) peaks in blood glucose levels.

b) They have poor diets rich in carbohydrate and they lack exercise.

Long-term effects and future trends

People who have had diabetes for a long time and whose blood glucose level is not tightly controlled are at risk of developing **long-term complications** – these include:

● **eye damage** (and blindness)

● **heart disease** and **strokes** (circulatory diseases)

● **kidney damage**.

The number of people who suffer diabetes is increasing rapidly and the cost of treatment is becoming very high. The large increase in the number of people with Type 2 diabetes is linked to poor diet and a lack of exercise.

Revision questions

Tested

1 State **two** ways in which reflexes differ from voluntary actions. **[2 marks]**

2 The diagram shows some seedlings that have light coming from one side only.

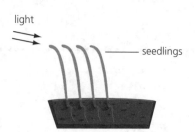

light

seedlings

   a) Name this growth response in plants. [1]

   b) Name the chemical inside the seedlings that causes this response. [1]

   c) Explain how this response benefits the seedlings. [2] **[4 marks]**

3 The diagram below represents the female reproductive system.

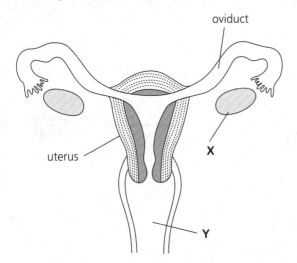

oviduct

uterus

X

Y

a) Name parts **X** and **Y**. [2]

b) Name the place where fertilisation takes place. [1]

c) State **one** change that takes place to the uterus during pregnancy. [1]

d) i) Describe the process of female sterilisation. [2]

  ii) Suggest why this method of contraception is usually not appropriate for younger women. [1]

  [7 marks]

4 The graph below shows how levels of oestrogen changes during the menstrual cycle.

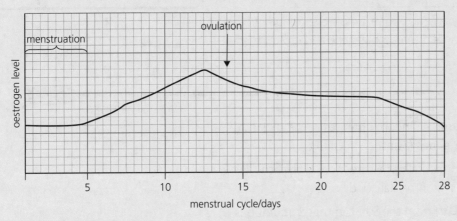

oestrogen level

menstruation

ovulation

5   10   15   20   25   28

menstrual cycle/days

a) i) What is the evidence that oestrogen stimulates ovulation. [1]

  ii) Name one other effect of oestrogen. [1]

b) i) Name one other hormone involved in controlling the menstrual cycle. [1]

  ii) Give one function of this hormone. [1] [4 marks]

5 a) Copy and complete the table by putting the symptoms and long-term effects of diabetes in the correct columns. Choose from:

eye damage   glucose in urine   thirst   stroke [2]

Symptom	Long-term effect

b) Give **three** reasons why the costs of treating diabetes are so high. [3] [5 marks]

Go online for the answers

Tested

4 Adaptation and variation

Living organisms that belong to the same species (type) resemble each other, but usually differ in a number of ways – these differences are called **variation**.

Variation

Revised

Variation can be:

- **genetic** – due to our genes
- **environmental** – due to the environment or lifestyle
- due to a combination of both – for example you have genes for a particular height, but your actual height reached depends on your health and diet.

Variation can be **continuous** or **discontinuous** as shown in the table below.

Variation	Description	Example
continuous	gradual change in a feature with no clearly distinct groups – no clear boundaries	height
discontinuous	individuals can be grouped into distinct groups easily with no overlap	tongue rolling

Exam tip

In exam questions continuous variation is often represented by a histogram and discontinuous variation by a bar chart.

Discontinuous variation is usually genetic – for example eye colour and blood group. Continuous variation is often both genetic and environmental.

Mutations

Revised

Variation can be due to **mutations** – random **changes** in the structure or number of **chromosomes** or **genes** (a change in DNA).

Although mutations can happen naturally, they are more likely if the living organism is exposed to certain environmental conditions.

For example, **ultraviolet** light (**UV**) from the Sun can trigger mutations leading to **skin cancer**. Cancer involves **uncontrolled cell division** that results in many more cells being produced than normal, causing a tumour.

Tanning (by the Sun or by using sunbeds) has some advantages, but also many disadvantages as shown in the table below.

Advantages	Disadvantages
helps us to make vitamin D	can cause sunburn
makes us feel good	can damage eyes
	can cause skin cancer

Overall, too much UV light can seriously damage health. We can reduce the damage by:

- avoiding midday and afternoon sunlight
- using sunscreen
- wearing a hat to protect the face and eyes
- limiting the time spent in UV light.

Down syndrome

Down syndrome is caused by a mutation. This involves a change in **chromosome numbers** – most mutations involve changes in the structure of genes or chromosomes. Individuals with Down syndrome have 47 rather than 46 chromosomes in each cell.

It is possible to tell if someone has Down syndrome by studying a **karyotype** – a diagram or photograph of all the chromosomes in a cell carefully laid out (usually in pairs) so that they can be counted.

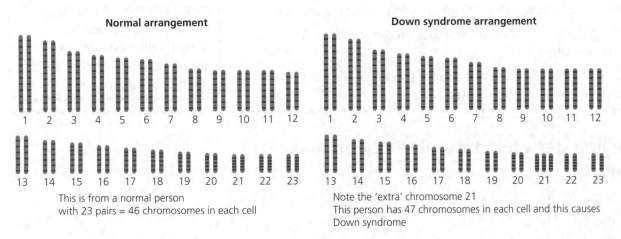

Normal arrangement

1 2 3 4 5 6 7 8 9 10 11 12
13 14 15 16 17 18 19 20 21 22 23

This is from a normal person
with 23 pairs = 46 chromosomes in each cell

Down syndrome arrangement

1 2 3 4 5 6 7 8 9 10 11 12
13 14 15 16 17 18 19 20 21 22 23

Note the 'extra' chromosome 21
This person has 47 chromosomes in each cell and this causes Down syndrome

↑ **Figure 4.1 Karyotypes showing different chromosome arrangements**

Natural selection

Revised

All living organisms are **adapted** for living in their normal environment. For example, a polar bear is camouflaged against the white snow and ice and its thick fur protects it against the cold. If organisms were not adapted they couldn't survive.

However, within any one species some organisms are better adapted to survive than others. The better-adapted organisms are more likely to survive than the less-well adapted ones – this is **natural selection**.

Example of natural selection

Pesticides are chemicals used to kill harmful insects. This example concerns mosquitoes.

- In many insect species some of the insects (<10%) are resistant (not harmed by) to pesticides because of a mutation.
- Most insects are not resistant and would be killed if they were sprayed by a pesticide.
- If a swarm of mosquitoes was sprayed with a pesticide then only the resistant ones would survive – all the non-resistant ones would be killed.

> **Exam tip**
>
> Natural selection has two key elements:
>
> - **difference between phenotypes** (e.g. some grey squirrels can run faster than others and escape from predators)
> - **differential survival** (e.g. the fastest squirrels survive and the slower ones get caught).

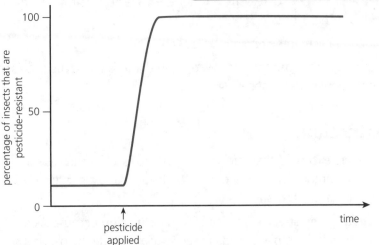

↑ **Figure 4.2 Pesticide resistance in mosquitoes**

Worked example

Using the example of pesticide resistance in mosquitoes, explain what is meant by:

a) variation within phenotypes

b) differential survival

c) natural selection.

Answer

a) Some mosquitoes are pesticide resistant and some are not.

b) The pesticide-resistant mosquitoes survive but the non-resistant ones are killed.

c) Only the best-adapted mosquitoes (pesticide-resistant ones) survive when pesticide is used.

Exam tip

Pesticide-resistant insects are already present (in small numbers) when a pesticide is used – the pesticide does not *cause* the development of pesticide resistance.

The link between natural selection and evolution

Natural selection was a key feature of Charles Darwin's work on evolution. Darwin summarised natural selection:

1 There is variation between individuals in a species.

2 If there is competition for resources there will be a struggle for existence.

3 The better-adapted individuals survive in this struggle.

4 This leads to survival of the fittest – these individuals are more likely to breed and pass their beneficial genes on to the next generation.

Darwin used his theory of natural selection to explain the process of **evolution**.

● Natural selection can explain how species have changed gradually over time in a process called evolution.

● This happens because certain features in the species are favoured – these have genes more likely to be passed on.

● Eventually the species may be very different from how it started out.

● Evolution is a continuing process – natural selection is always happening and all species change very gradually over a long time period.

There are a number of reasons why not everyone accepts the theory of evolution. These include:

● it contradicts some religious beliefs

● the very long time scales involved mean that it is very difficult to see evolution actually happening.

Extinction

Species are **extinct** if there are no living examples left – such as the woolly mammoth and the dinosaurs. We know that extinct species once existed because of **fossils**.

An **endangered species** is one at **risk of extinction** because there are so few left. Examples of endangered species include the panda, the rhinoceros and some species of large cat.

Although extinction can happen naturally, man has been responsible for the extinction of thousands of species and has put many more at risk. However, man also has the potential to save endangered species by stopping them becoming extinct.

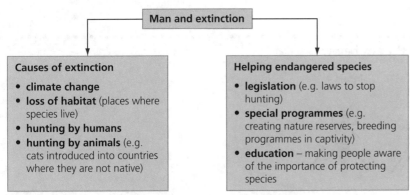

↑ **Figure 4.3 Man's role in causing and preventing extinction**

Worked example

African mountain gorillas are endangered because their mountain forest habitat is being destroyed as man removes the trees to create land for farming, as well as wood for sale. The gorillas are also at risk from illegal poaching (hunting) by man. Part of their habitat has been made a national park to preserve their habitat.

a) Explain the difference between 'endangered' and 'extinct'.

b) Suggest **two** ways in which the gorillas can be further protected.

Answer

a) Endangered species are at risk of extinction but not yet extinct.

b) Any **two** from: extend the area of the national park; have patrols to prevent poaching/hunting; starting special breeding programmes.

Classification of living organisms
Revised

Classification is the naming of organisms and their allocation to particular groups.

Organisms are classified in groups using a range of features such as number of limbs or presence/absence of eyes.

Important reasons for classifying organisms include:

● previously unknown organisms can be allocated to a group

● makes it possible to identify any organism

● helps in studying relationships between different groups of organisms.

Keys can be used to identify any living organism.

Using a key

There are many different types of key, but they all work in a similar way to the example below.

Worked example

Identify the insects in the diagram using the key below.

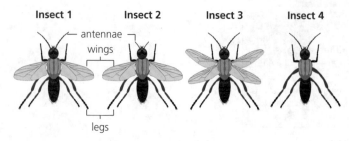

Insect 1   Insect 2   Insect 3   Insect 4

antennae
wings
legs

1 Wings present? Yes – go to 2; No wings = species **W**

2 Two wings? Yes – go to 3; Four wings = species **X**

3 Antennae longer than head? Yes – species **Y**; Antennae shorter than head? Yes – species **Z**

Answer

insect **1** = species **Y**; insect **2** = species **Z**; insect **3** = species **X**; insect **4** = species **W**

Revision questions

Tested

1 **a)** Explain what is meant by 'discontinuous variation'. [1]

   b) Give **one** example of discontinuous variation. [1]   [2 marks]

2 **a)** Describe precisely what a mutation is. [1]

   b) Give the name of **one** environmental factor that can cause mutations. [1]

   c) Give the name of **one** condition caused by a change in chromosome number. [1] [3 marks]

3 In a typical pasture there may be a few plants that are gene resistant to high levels of copper in the soil. In these conditions, normal grasses grow better than the copper-resistant variety. However, in areas where the soil is contaminated with copper, the copper-resistant variety may make up over 90 per cent of the plants present. Explain how the increase of copper-resistant plants in contaminated soil demonstrates natural selection.   [3 marks]

4 The panda is at risk of extinction. It feeds on bamboo and a major reason for the panda becoming endangered is the reduction in bamboo forests. Suggest **two** ways in which man can help panda numbers to recover.   [2 marks]

Go online for the answers

Online

5 Disease and body defences

Pasteur and contamination

Before **Louis Pasteur's** famous experiment in 1861, people did not know what caused food to go bad.

Using his 'swan-neck' flasks, he was able to show that food going bad (contamination) was caused by **microorganisms (microbes)**. Figure 5.1 shows apparatus similar to that used by Pasteur. The **key conclusion** of his work was that contamination occurs only if microorganisms can gain access to food.

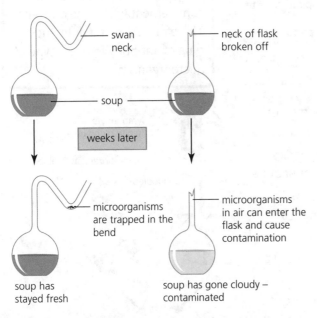

↑ **Figure 5.1 Pasteur's swan-neck experiment**

Exam tip

It is important to control variables – this ensures that a fair test is carried out, which makes the investigation valid.

Exam tip

You should know that scientists were able to conclude from Pasteur's experiment that many illnesses are also caused by microorganisms getting into the body.

Worked example

a) It was important to wash the apparatus thoroughly and boil the soup at the start of Pasteur's investigation. Explain why.

b) State **three** controlled variables (things that must have been kept the same) in Pasteur's investigation.

Answer

a) For the test to be valid it is important that there were no microorganisms in the apparatus or soup at the start.

b) The same type of broth was used; the flasks were kept at the same temperature; they were left for the same length of time.

Types of microorganism

There are different types of microorganism that make food go bad or that cause disease – they are shown in the table below.

Microorganism type	Examples of diseases caused by microorganisms
bacteria	gonorrhoea, chlamydia, salmonella, tuberculosis (TB)
viruses	HIV leading to AIDS, cold, flu, polio, chickenpox, rubella
fungi	athlete's foot, thrush

The body defends against disease in a number of ways.

The body defences

These involve both stopping harmful microorganisms gaining entry to the body and destroying them in the blood.

1 The first stage of defence is stopping microorganisms from entering the body.

Skin	barrier that stops microorganisms entering the body
Mucous membranes	thin membranes in the nose and respiratory system that trap and expel microbes
Clotting	closes wounds quickly to form a barrier that stops microorganisms gaining entry (also prevents loss of blood)

2 The role of **white blood cells** is to destroy microorganisms that have entered the body. There are two main ways this happens:

a) **Lymphocytes** are white blood cells that produce antibodies when microorganisms enter the blood. Protection by antibodies involves:

- microorganisms have special 'marker' chemicals on their surface called **antigens**

- these antigens cause the lymphocytes (white blood cells) to produce **antibodies**

- the antibodies are complementary in shape (like a lock and key) to the antigens

- they latch on to the antigens (microorganisms) linking them together

- this **immobilises** (clumps) the microorganisms and they then can be destroyed.

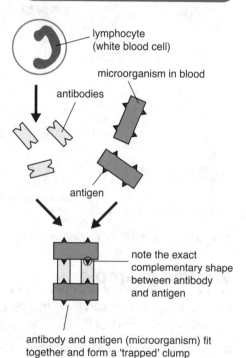

↑ Figure 5.2 How antibodies work

b) Once the microorganisms are clumped together, they are destroyed by a second type of white blood cell – the **phagocytes**. This process is called **phagocytosis**.

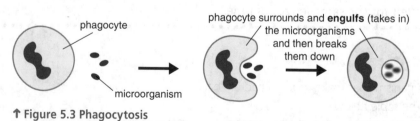

↑ Figure 5.3 Phagocytosis

Active immunity

Active immunity is achieved by the body making its own antibodies. This is how we recover from most diseases we catch.

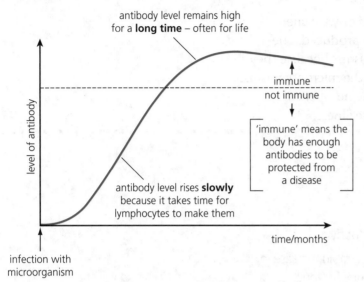

↑ **Figure 5.4 Active immunity through recovering from a disease**

Vaccinations are another way of getting active immunity. A vaccination is an injection of dead or weakened microorganisms – the way vaccinations work is explained in Figure 5.5.

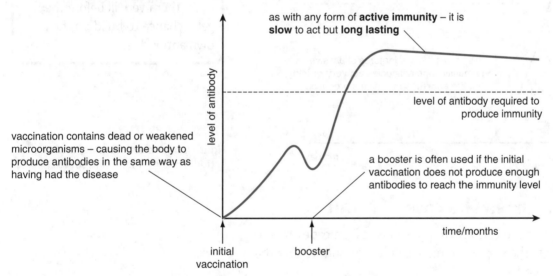

↑ **Figure 5.5 Active immunity by vaccination**

Some key features about vaccinations are explained below.

● The microorganisms in the vaccination fluid must be dead or weakened – otherwise they would give the person the disease that the vaccination is trying to stop.

● You need a different type of vaccination for each disease. This is because you need antibodies that are complementary to (match) the antigens on the disease-causing microorganism.

● You do not always need booster vaccinations – if the initial vaccination causes the antibody levels to rise high enough a booster is not needed.

Worked example

Explain how vaccination protects against disease.

Answer

The vaccination fluid contains antigens (on dead or weakened microorganisms) – these cause antibodies to be produced. The antibodies latch on to the antigens (microorganisms) because they are complementary in shape – this immobilises the microorganisms. They are then destroyed by phagocytosis and the numbers of microorganisms do not get high enough to cause illness.

Passive immunity

In **passive immunity**:

● we are given ready-made antibodies by injection

● the antibodies are not produced by the patient's body.

Figure 5.6 shows that passive immunity can provide a rapid increase in antibody levels, but the body does not remain immune for long.

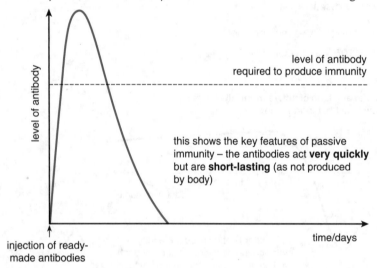

level of antibody required to produce immunity

this shows the key features of passive immunity – the antibodies act **very quickly** but are **short-lasting** (as not produced by body)

level of antibody

injection of ready-made antibodies

time/days

← Figure 5.6 Passive immunity and the injection of ready-made antibodies

Are vaccines safe? The case of MMR

The **MMR** vaccination protects against three diseases – measles, mumps and rubella. However, there has been more controversy surrounding this vaccination than any other.

This is the story of MMR:

1 Before 1998 more than 90% of children were vaccinated with the MMR vaccination.

2 In 1998 some research suggested that the MMR vaccination could cause autism.

3 After 1998 the percentage of children being vaccinated decreased for a number of years.

4 Later research showed that there is not a link between the MMR vaccination and autism.

5 The number of children being vaccinated now has risen again to over 90%.

Scientists now agree that there is not a link between the MMR vaccination and autism.

Antibiotics are chemicals that kill bacteria.

The discovery of penicillin – the first antibiotic

In 1928 Alexander Fleming was growing bacteria on plates containing a nutrient jelly (agar).

One of his plates became infected by a fungus. Fleming noticed that bacteria could not grow in the region around where the fungus was growing.

The conclusion was something (a chemical) was spreading from the fungus and killing the bacteria.

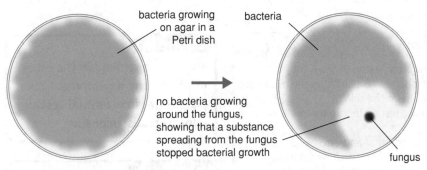

↑ **Figure 5.7 Fleming's discovery**

Many years later, other scientists were able to make a pure form of this substance that could kill bacteria. It was **penicillin** – the first antibiotic to be made.

Bacterial resistance to antibiotics

Sometimes bacteria can evolve (change) so that antibiotics no longer have an effect, as explained here.

1 Bacteria can **mutate**.

2 Their DNA changes and the bacteria develop new properties.

3 This can make them **resistant** to antibiotics.

4 Antibiotics will not work against these particular bacteria – or cure diseases caused by them.

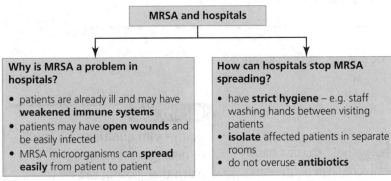

↑ **Figure 5.8 MRSA (superbugs) and hospitals**

Epidemics and pandemics

Revised

Infectious disease can affect many people and these two terms describe widespread infection.

- **Epidemic** – describes the rapid spread of a disease (e.g. flu) through a town or small region such as Northern Ireland with many people becoming infected.
- **Pandemic** – describes the rapid spread of disease on a wider scale, such as through many countries with many more people affected.

> **Exam tip**
>
> Epidemics and pandemics are more likely to happen if the disease-causing microorganisms:
> - are spread from person to person easily
> - mutate – previously successful vaccinations may no longer work.

Development of medicines

Revised

Medicines and medical drugs have to pass through a number of stages before they can be prescribed to the public.

Stage	What happens	Comment
in-vitro testing	testing on living cells in laboratory	• drugs are tested to see if they can combat disease and that the drug does not harm the cell • allows testing before use on living organisms • an initial 'trial-and-error' process • expensive because it needs highly-trained scientists and involves expensive equipment
animal testing	testing on animals to check how it works on whole animals	**Benefits** • avoids testing on humans at this stage • can check for side-effects on living organisms **Disadvantages** • animals are different to humans so the drug may react differently • raises ethical issues
clinical trials	testing on small numbers of volunteers and then patients	Testing for: • how effective the drug is at doing what it is meant to do • side-effects
licensing	the drug is licensed (given governmental approval)	• it can be used in treatment of the public

> **Exam tip**
>
> You should remember the order in which drug development takes place – *in-vitro*; **animal testing**; **clinical trials**; **licensing**.

> **Exam tip**
>
> Drug development is very **expensive**. The table states why *in-vitro* testing is expensive, but the other stages are expensive too – e.g. cost of keeping animals, payments to volunteers.

Other drugs

Revised

Alcohol, nicotine (in cigarettes), cannabis and cocaine are drugs that can harm the body.

Alcohol

Many people can drink small amounts of alcohol without causing harm. However, drinking too much (especially binge-drinking) can harm both the **individual** and **society** as shown in the table in Figure 5.9 on the next page.

> **Exam tip**
>
> Many exam questions ask you to distinguish between the harm that alcohol can do to individuals (the person) and also to society.

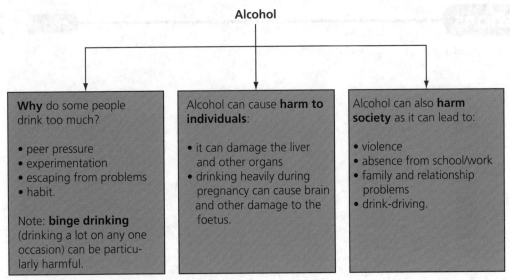

↑ Figure 5.9 Alcohol and its effects

There are many ways to **reduce the harm** caused by alcohol:

● drink less – e.g. drink low-alcohol drinks

● drink on fewer occasions – e.g. not during the week

● education – understand about units and the problems alcohol can cause

● never drink and drive

● do not drink alcohol until you reach the legal age limit.

Smoking

Smoking can seriously damage health as summarised in the table.

Substance in cigarette smoke	Harmful effect(s)
tar	causes bronchitis (narrowing of airways in lungs), emphysema and lung cancer
nicotine	addictive and affects the heart rate
carbon monoxide	combines with red blood cells to reduce the oxygen-carrying capacity of the blood

Illegal drugs

Cannabis and cocaine are two of the most common illegal drugs.

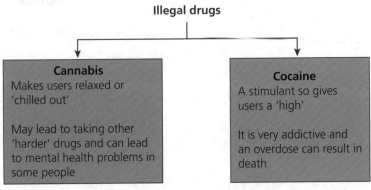

↑ Figure 5.10 Illegal drugs – cannabis and cocaine

1 The following apparatus was set up to investigate contamination in food.

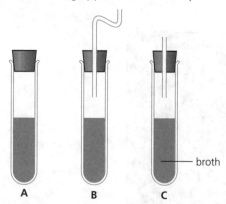

broth

A   B   C

a) Which tube(s) (**A**, **B** or **C**) will contain contaminated broth after 10 days? Explain your answer. [3]

b) State **two** things that must be done to ensure that the results are valid (fair test). [2]   **[5 marks]**

2 Give **one** similarity and **one** difference between active and passive immunity.   **[2 marks]**

3 Mary went to her doctor because she was suffering from a sore throat caused by a bacterial infection. Explain why the doctor gave her an antibiotic rather than a vaccination.   **[2 marks]**

4 a) i) Describe what is meant by 'in-vitro testing'. [1]

      ii) Suggest why it is so expensive. [1]

   b) Apart from ethical considerations, give **one** argument for and **one** argument against animal testing. [2]

   c) i) What is meant by the term 'side-effect'? [1]

      ii) Suggest why a drug could be licensed for use, even though it has some side-effects. [1]   **[6 marks]**

5 John would like to give up smoking but finds it very hard to stop.

   a) Name the chemical in cigarette smoke that makes it difficult for John to stop. [1]

   b) Explain how the carbon monoxide in cigarette smoke can lead to smoker having a shortage of energy. [3]   **[4 marks]**

Go online for the answers   Online

6 Human activity on Earth

It is important to strike a balance between population/economic growth and protecting/conserving the Earth. Growth needs to be sustainable – **sustainable** means that we do not harm our environment or deplete our resources.

The human population

Revised

The growth of the human population is in danger of putting the planet at risk – it is not sustainable.

Figure 6.1 shows how the human population changed between the years 1750 and 2000.

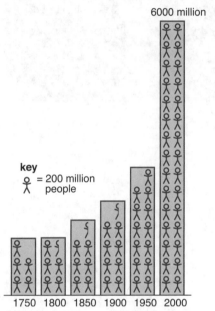

↑ Figure 6.1 The growth of the human population

> ### Exam tip
>
> You need to know why human population growth causes the harmful effects listed below. For example, woodland habitats are destroyed to create more room for housing and agriculture.

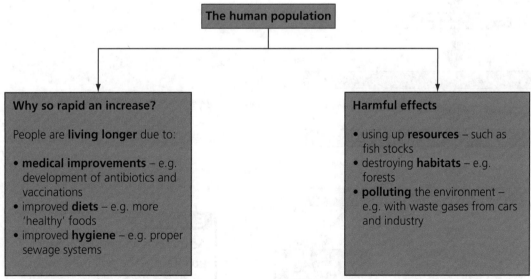

↑ Figure 6.2 Human population growth – causes and effects

Managing resources

Using fish stocks as an example, many types of fish have become endangered because of over-fishing. There are many measures in place to encourage sustainable fishing and conserving fish stocks – Figure 6.3 shows some.

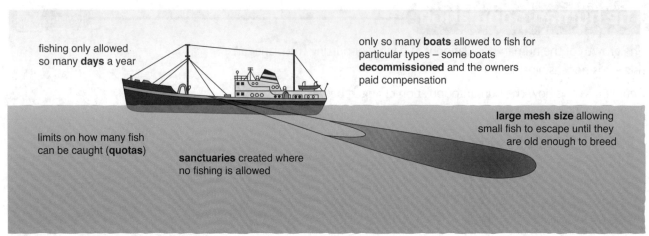

fishing only allowed so many **days** a year

only so many **boats** allowed to fish for particular types – some boats **decommissioned** and the owners paid compensation

large mesh size allowing small fish to escape until they are old enough to breed

limits on how many fish can be caught (**quotas**)

sanctuaries created where no fishing is allowed

↑ **Figure 6.3 Conserving fish stocks**

Pollution

All living organisms produce waste – **pollution** is producing so much waste that it harms the environment. Pollution affects the air, the land and the water.

Air pollution – we pollute the air (atmosphere) by producing too much **carbon dioxide**, mainly due to burning too much **fossil fuel** (see the next section). Burning fossil fuels also produces **acid rain.**

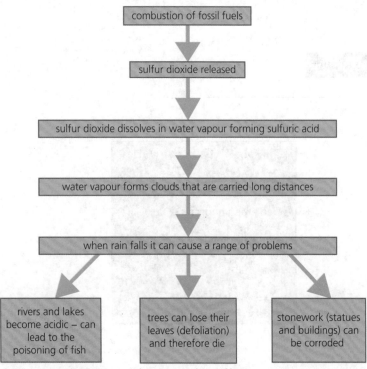

combustion of fossil fuels

↓

sulfur dioxide released

↓

sulfur dioxide dissolves in water vapour forming sulfuric acid

↓

water vapour forms clouds that are carried long distances

↓

when rain falls it can cause a range of problems

rivers and lakes become acidic – can lead to the poisoning of fish

trees can lose their leaves (defoliation) and therefore die

stonework (statues and buildings) can be corroded

↑ **Figure 6.4 Acid rain production and its effects**

> **Exam tip**
>
> Acid rain is an unusual form of pollution – the polluting country can be well away from the countries that suffer the effects.

The effects of acid rain can be reduced by:

- using **filters** in the chimneys of power stations and in other industries that burn a lot of fossil fuel
- using **alternative fuels** such as solar or wind power.

Land pollution – too much household waste ends up in **landfill** sites; these use up valuable land, are unsightly and attract vermin.

We can reduce the need for landfill sites by **reducing** the use of materials, **reusing** them or **recycling** used materials.

Water pollution – sewage and slurry from farms are very rich in nutrients, particularly **nitrates**. If nitrates drain into surrounding waterways they can cause harm (eutrophication) as described in Figure 6.5.

We can **reduce** nitrate pollution by:

- only spreading sewage and slurry (fertiliser) on farmland during the growing season
- not spreading it on sloping ground near waterways or when the land is wet
- making sure that sewage and slurry are properly stored and cannot leak into surrounding land/water.

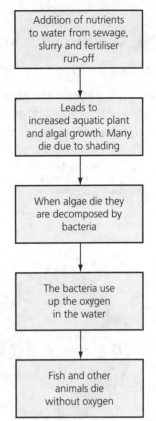

↑ **Figure 6.5 The effect of nitrate pollution in water**

Global warming   Revised ▢

Global warming means that the Earth's atmosphere is heating up.

The carbon cycle

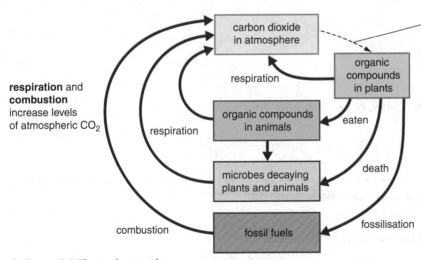

↑ **Figure 6.6 The carbon cycle**

Over the last 150 years there have been two major changes that affect the carbon cycle:

- increased **combustion** of fossil fuels
- increased **deforestation.**

These changes mean that the carbon cycle has become **unbalanced**, leading to an **increase** in carbon dioxide in the atmosphere.

Exam tip

Deforestation is the removal of trees – usually to provide more land for agriculture or housing. This means that there is less photosynthesis happening and, therefore, less carbon dioxide being taken out of the atmosphere.

Increasing carbon dioxide levels and global warming

Carbon dioxide forms a layer in the atmosphere (greenhouse layer/blanket) that traps heat escaping (**greenhouse effect**) warming the atmosphere up (**global warming**) as shown in Figure 6.7.

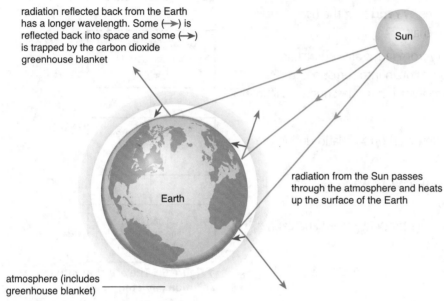

radiation reflected back from the Earth has a longer wavelength. Some (→) is reflected back into space and some (→) is trapped by the carbon dioxide greenhouse blanket

Sun

radiation from the Sun passes through the atmosphere and heats up the surface of the Earth

Earth

atmosphere (includes greenhouse blanket)

↑ Figure 6.7 The greenhouse effect

The **effects** of global warming include:

- climate change – more storms and droughts
- polar ice caps melting
- increased flooding
- more land becoming desert.

Global warming can be **slowed down** by:

- planting more trees
- reducing deforestation
- burning less fossil fuels by using alternative fuels or being more energy efficient.

Worked example

a) Explain the link between increasing atmospheric carbon dioxide levels and the increased flooding of low-lying land.

b) Suggest **one** reason why most people now accept that global warming is a man-made problem.

Answer

a) ● Increasing carbon dioxide levels build up in a (greenhouse) layer that traps heat escaping from the atmosphere.
   ● The Earth's atmosphere / the Earth heats up.
   ● Melting ice caps causes flooding.

b) There is more evidence now – e.g. polar ice-cap data, meteorological data / better monitoring technology.

The history of the Earth's atmosphere

Although carbon dioxide levels are changing now, the proportions of other gases in the atmosphere have also changed through time.

Animal life is only possible because plant life and **photosynthesis** evolved, causing **oxygen** levels to rise.

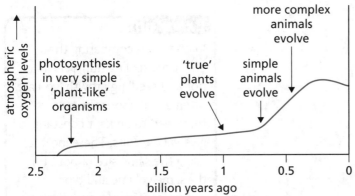

↑ Figure 6.8 The changing levels of atmospheric oxygen

> **Exam tip**
>
> Animals need plants to provide oxygen and as a food source.

> **Exam tip**
>
> Complex animals evolved less than 0.5 billion years ago because by then the oxygen levels had risen high enough to support the high respiration rates needed.

The nitrogen cycle

Plants obtain nitrogen in the form of **nitrates** from the soil. It is needed to make **proteins**.

Figure 6.9 shows how nitrogen is cycled through plants, animals and bacteria in the soil.

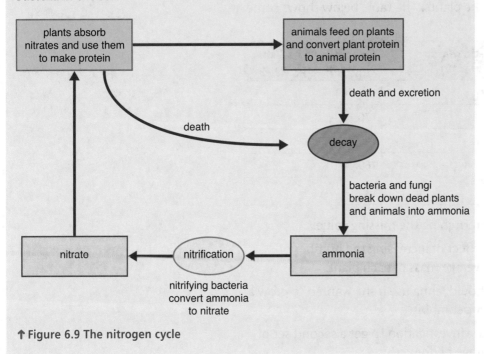

↑ Figure 6.9 The nitrogen cycle

Competition between living things

Living organisms compete with each other for resources.

Competition among plant seedlings

For example, the more seedlings that are planted in a pot, the smaller the average mass of each seedling. This is because the seedlings are competing for light, space, nutrients and water.

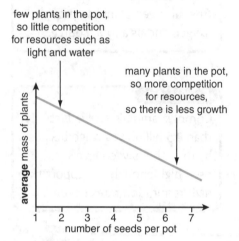

↑ Figure 6.10 Competition in plants

> **Exam tip**
>
> In questions comparing the effect of seedling numbers in a pot and seedling growth, you are often asked about the factors that need to be kept constant to give valid results. These include using the same size of pot, using the same volume and type of compost, giving the pots the same environmental conditions – e.g. the same amount of water, the same light, the same temperature.

Worked example

Jenna carried out an investigation to check if the number of plants in a pot affected the growth of the plants. The table below shows some of the results.

Number of plants in the pot	Average mass of each plant/g	Total mass of all the plants in each pot/g
5	20	100
10	17	170
15	13	195
20	8	160
25	5	

a) Complete the table by determining the missing value.

b) Describe and explain the effect of increasing the number of plants in the pot on the average mass of each plant.

c) Which planting density should Jenna use if she wanted to grow a large crop to help feed her pet rabbit?

d) Jenna decided to repeat the investigation to get a second set of results. Explain the advantage of doing this.

Answer

a) $25 \times 5 = 125$

b) As the number of plants in the pot increases, the average mass of each plant decreases

c) 15 plants per pot; this gives the highest total mass

d) Increases reliability

Competitive invasive species

These are species that can compete so well that they can damage habitats and other species.

Competitive invasive species usually have a number of features in common:

- they are **not native** – they have been introduced by man from other countries
- they **spread rapidly**
- they **out-compete native species** – causing them to reduce in number or become extinct.

Two examples are:

- **grey squirrels** – introduced from America; they have spread rapidly causing a decrease in number of native red squirrels.
- **rhododendron** – since being introduced this plant species has spread rapidly; dense, evergreen leaves stop other species from growing underneath it.

Conservation

Revised ☐

Conservation means managing the environment in a sustainable way. When managing the environment it is important to monitor changes to know what is happening.

Monitoring change in the environment

We can use living (**biotic**) or non-living (**abiotic**) factors.

Abiotic (non-living) factors are important for monitoring global warming. They include:

- carbon dioxide levels
- size of ice fields and water levels
- climate change.

Biotic (living) factors are important too. **Lichens** are sensitive plants that can be used to monitor pollution. Lichens will grow only in areas where pollution levels are low; they cannot grow in areas that have high levels of pollution.

Growing willow for biofuel

We can conserve fossil fuels and reduce carbon emissions into the atmosphere by using willow as a biofuel.

- Willow is renewable (unlike fossil fuels) because it can be regrown every 3 years.
- When growing it uses up carbon dioxide in photosynthesis.
- When used as a fuel it releases carbon dioxide (but no more than it had already taken in).

> **Exam tip**
>
> Willow can be described as 'carbon-neutral' because it neither adds to nor reduces atmospheric carbon dioxide levels.

Maintaining biodiversity

Biodiversity refers to the range of species (different types of living organisms) in an area.

One way of maintaining a high biodiversity is to develop nature reserves.

Nature reserves help to protect and conserve the environment by:

● **restricting access** to fragile habitats, or where very rare species are found

● **managing the habitat** – e.g. by removing invasive species such as rhododendron

● **educating the public** about nature and the benefits of conservation.

Revision questions

Tested

1 Suggest why acid rain is referred to as an international problem. **[1 mark]**

2 The following diagram shows the role coal (a fossil fuel) plays in the carbon cycle.

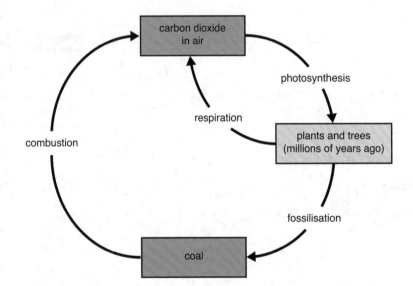

a) Name the process that lowers carbon dioxide levels in the atmosphere. [1]

b) Name the process that does not affect carbon dioxide levels. [1]

c) Using the diagram and your knowledge, explain what causes global warming. [3]

d) State **one** harmful effect of global warming. [1] **[6 marks]**

3   The graph below shows the relationship between the number of lichen plants on beech trees and their distance from a town in 1960 and 2010. During the investigation the number of lichen plants on tree trunks between the heights of 1 and 3 metres was counted. This was done for 5 trees at 5 km distances from the town.

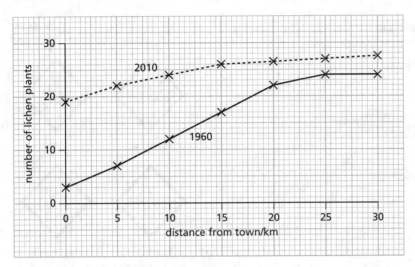

a) State **two** trends shown by the graph. [2]

b) Suggest an explanation for **one** of the trends. [1]

c) Use the information provided to state **two** things that were done to ensure that the results were valid. [2]

d) State **one** thing that could be done to increase the reliability of the results. [1]   **[6 marks]**

4   When adding fertiliser (e.g. slurry) to plants or crops it is important that it is not sprayed on sloping ground close to waterways or when the ground is very wet. Explain why this is important.   **[3 marks]**

5   Nature reserves help protect biodiversity.

a) What is meant by biodiversity? [1]

b) For an area to be selected as a nature reserve, it usually has a number of features. Suggest **one** feature that a nature reserve should have. [1]

c) Describe and explain the effect that rhododendron will have on the biodiversity of a woodland floor. [3]   **[5 marks]**

Go online for the answers   Online

7 Acids and bases

Many chemicals (including acids and bases) can cause harm – they are hazards. Hazard symbols are used to identify products that are hazardous.

Hazard symbols

Revised

Figure 7.1 shows the main hazard symbols.

This table explains each hazard.

Hazard	Explanation
corrosive	can burn the skin
toxic	can cause harm by poisoning
explosive	can explode
flammable	can catch fire easily

Hazard symbols are used because:

- they have greater visual impact than words
- they are easily recognised
- they can be understood irrespective of language.

corrosive

toxic

explosive

flammable

↑ Figure 7.1 Hazard symbols

Exam tip

If asked to name a hazard represented by the toxic symbol, you must state 'toxic' – 'poisoning' does not usually gain credit because this is its effect.

Acids and bases

Revised

A substance with pH 7 is described as having a neutral pH. **Acids** have a pH lower than 7; **soluble bases (alkalis)** have a pH higher than 7.

Acids and alkalis/bases can be useful in the home.

For example:

- vinegar is acidic – it contains ethanoic acid
- lemon juice is acidic – it contains citric acid
- baking soda is a base – it contains sodium hydrogencarbonate
- *Milk of Magnesia* is an alkali – it contains the base magnesium hydroxide
- many cleaning products are alkalis – they contain ammonia
- many oven and drain cleaners are alkalis – they contain sodium hydroxide.

Indicators and pH

Indicators can tell us whether a substance is neutral, acid or alkali. They usually do this by having different colours when in different solutions.

Natural indicators are those that occur naturally. Beetroot, blackcurrant and red cabbage plants contain dyes that change colour depending on whether they are in acidic, neutral or alkaline solutions.

Natural indicators can be made as follows:

1 Chop the plant or leaves into small pieces and put in a mortar.

2 Add a small amount of water.

3 Use a pestle to grind the mixture to release the dye.

4 The dye and the water form a solution that can be filtered into a small beaker.

This solution can act as an indicator because it turns different colours when added to neutral, acidic or alkaline solutions.

Universal indicator can do more than a natural indicator. It can tell us the **strength** of an alkali or an acid. It will turn a different colour in a weak acid (e.g. citric acid) than it will in a strong acid (e.g. hydrochloric acid).

The pH scale runs from 1 to 14 with 1–6 indicating acid, 7 neutral and 8–14 alkali. The closer an acid is to pH 1, the stronger an acid it is; the closer an alkali is to pH 14, the stronger an alkali it is. The table below shows the colours of universal indicator over a range of pH values.

pH	1	2	3	4	5	6	7	8	9	10	11	12	13	14
universal indicator colour	red	red	orange	orange	yellow	yellow	green	green/blue	green/blue	blue	blue	purple	purple	purple
strength	strong acid	strong acid	weak acid	weak acid	weak acid	weak acid	neutral	weak alkali	weak alkali	weak alkali	weak alkali	strong alkali	strong alkali	strong alkali

There are other ways of measuring the pH of a solution:

● **pH paper** is filter paper strips soaked in universal indicator and allowed to dry – when dipped in a solution it changes colour in the same way as universal indicator does.

● a **pH sensor** is an electronic device that gives a numerical value (rather than a colour) for pH – connecting the sensor to a data logger allows pH values to be transferred to a computer.

A pH sensor has a number of advantages:

● numerical readings from pH sensors are more accurate than visually estimating colours – the pH value may be given to two decimal places

● a data logger can record continuous values – this is important when recording pH changes over a period of time.

Neutralisation

When an alkali is added to an acid, the pH changes from a low value (the value of the acid) to a higher pH value.

The reaction is described as **neutralisation** – Figure 7.2 shows how to carry out a neutralisation reaction.

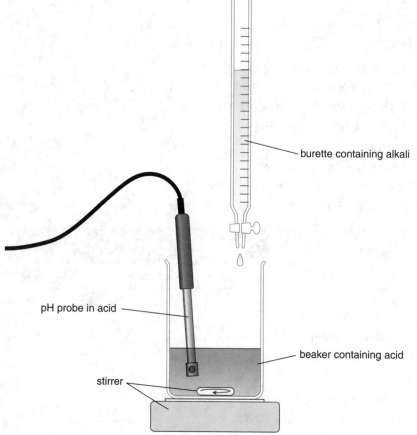

burette containing alkali

pH probe in acid

beaker containing acid

stirrer

↑ **Figure 7.2 A neutralisation reaction**

The type of graph produced when adding an alkali (e.g. sodium hydroxide) to an acid (e.g. hydrochloric acid) is shown in Figure 7.3.

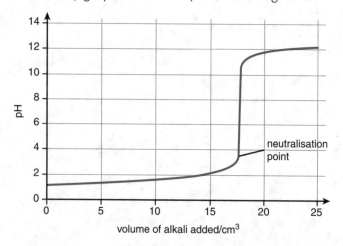

↑ **Figure 7.3 Graph of pH changes in a neutralisation reaction**

Chemical formulae and neutralisation

Neutralisation is the reaction between an acid and an alkali (base), forming a **salt** and **water**.

In the example of neutralisation shown on the previous page:

sodium hydroxide + hydrochloric acid → sodium chloride + water
    (alkali)   (acid)   (salt)

- the first part of the name of the salt is the same ('sodium') as the metal in the alkali (base)
- the second part of the name of the salt is 'chloride' because it comes from the acid.

Note: If sulfuric acid is used the salt is a 'sulfate' – for example if sulfuric acid is added to sodium hydroxide then the products are sodium sulfate and water.

You need to be familiar with and be able to recognise common chemical formulae. The formulae for the substances used in the example of neutralisation above are:

- NaOH – sodium hydroxide
- HCl – hydrochloric acid
- NaCl – sodium chloride
- H_2O – water

You need to be able to work out:

- the number of **elements** in a chemical formula. For example NaCl has two elements – Na (sodium) and Cl (chlorine). Similarly, NaOH has three different elements – Na (sodium), O (oxygen) and H (hydrogen).
- the number of **atoms** – NaCl has one atom of sodium (Na) and one of chlorine (Cl). However, water (H_2O) has two atoms of hydrogen and one of oxygen.

> **Exam tip**
>
> When working out numbers of atoms you should remember that if the number is a subscript (small and low down) it refers to the element immediately before it. If it is normal size it refers to all the elements after it. For example, in sodium hydrogencarbonate ($2NaHCO_3$) there are two sodium (Na) atoms, two hydrogen (H) atoms, two carbon (C) atoms and six oxygen (O) atoms (2×3).

Symbol equations using chemical formula

The symbol equation for the reaction between sodium hydroxide and hydrochloric acid is

$$NaOH + HCl \rightarrow NaCl + H_2O$$

This equation is balanced because there are the same numbers of each type of atom on each side.

There is one Na atom on each side and there are two H atoms on the left and two on the right (H_2).

When writing symbol equations it is often necessary to balance the sides – you need to make the numbers of atoms on each side match. Balancing equations will be covered in a later section.

Acid indigestion

The human stomach contains hydrochloric acid – a strong acid with a pH around 2. This acid kills microorganisms reaching the stomach in food and also helps digestion. However, too much acid can cause acid indigestion. People can take substances that neutralise excess stomach acid and cure the indigestion.

Indigestion tablets contain weak bases such as oxides or hydroxides – e.g. magnesium hydroxide – and/or carbonates – e.g. sodium hydrogencarbonate.

If we use sodium hydrogencarbonate (baking soda) as an antacid the reaction is:

sodium hydrogencarbonate + hydrochloric acid $\rightarrow$ sodium chloride + carbon dioxide + water

This reaction neutralises the excess hydrochloric acid and the carbon dioxide gas escapes out of the body as a burp (wind).

The balanced symbol equation for the reaction is:

$$NaHCO_3 + HCl \rightarrow NaCl + CO_2 + H_2O$$

Worked example

Using the example of sodium hydroxide neutralising hydrochloric acid for reference, work out the word equation for *Milk of Magnesia* (contains magnesium hydroxide) curing acid indigestion.

Answer

magnesium hydroxide + hydrochloric acid $\rightarrow$ magnesium chloride + water

Note again:

- the first part of the name of the salt is the same as the metal in the base
- the second part of the name of the salt is 'chloride' because it comes from hydrochloric acid.

The balanced symbol equation for magnesium hydroxide curing acid indigestion is:

$$Mg(OH)_2 + 2HCl \rightarrow MgCl_2 + 2H_2O$$

The '2' before the HCl and before the H_2O are balancing numbers – they are needed to balance the numbers of atoms on each side. '2HCl' means that there are two hydrogen atoms and two chlorine atoms. Similarly in '2H$_2$O' there are four hydrogen atoms and two oxygen atoms.

The brackets around and the '$_2$' after the 'OH' means that there are two oxygen atoms and two hydrogen atoms.

Worked example

Calcium carbonate reacts with hydrochloric acid in the stomach to produce calcium chloride, carbon dioxide and water.

Balance the symbol equation for this reaction:

$$CaCO_3 + HCl \rightarrow CaCl_2 + CO_2 + H_2O$$

Answer

- there is one calcium (Ca) atom on each side – no balancing needed
- there is one carbon atom (C) on each side – no balancing needed
- there are three oxygen (O) atoms on each side – no balancing needed
- there is one hydrogen (H) atom on the left and two on the right (balancing needed)
- there is one chlorine atom (Cl) on the left and two on the right (balancing needed)
- the equation can be balanced by putting a '2' before the HCl on the left – remember this means there are two 'H' atoms and 2 'Cl' atoms

The balanced symbol equation is:

$$CaCO_3 + 2HCl \rightarrow CaCl_2 + CO_2 + H_2O$$

When carbonates or hydrogencarbonates are used to cure acid indigestion, carbon dioxide is produced, which can build up in the stomach causing 'wind'. The earlier worked example shows that this does not happen with antacids such as magnesium hydroxide because carbon dioxide is not produced.

You can test for carbon dioxide gas using limewater. If baking soda (sodium hydrogencarbonate) and hydrochloric acid are mixed as shown in Figure 7.4, the carbon dioxide bubbles through the limewater turning it from colourless to milky (cloudy).

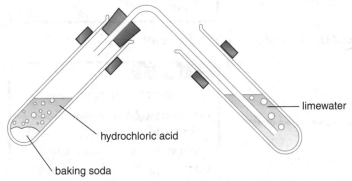

limewater

hydrochloric acid

baking soda

↑ **Figure 7.4 Using limewater to test for carbon dioxide**

Exam tip

Limewater is a test for carbon dioxide because carbon dioxide is the only gas that turns it from colourless to milky/cloudy.

Neutralising acidic soil

Many crops will not grow in soils that are too acidic. Most plants grow best if the soil is neutral or slightly alkaline. Farmers can neutralise acidic soils by adding lime (calcium hydroxide) or limestone (calcium carbonate).

The release of carbon dioxide from carbonates

We have covered baking soda (sodium hydrogencarbonate) and its role as an antacid in earlier sections but you need to be aware of some of its other reactions and uses.

Baking soda

If baking soda is heated it is broken down as shown here:

sodium hydrogencarbonate $\xrightarrow{\text{heat}}$ **sodium carbonate + carbon dioxide + water**

The balanced symbol equation for this reaction is:

$$2NaHCO_3 \rightarrow Na_2CO_3 + CO_2 + H_2O$$

There are:

- two Na atoms on the left ('2Na') and two on the right ('Na$_2$')
- two H atoms on the left and two on the right
- two C atoms on the left and two on the right
- six O atoms on the left and six on the right.

> **Exam tip**
>
> If a formula is written like '2NaHCO$_3$' this means that each atom (Na, H, C and O) are multiplied by two. The O is also multiplied by 3 to give six O atoms altogether.

When heat is used to break down a compound (e.g. sodium hydrogencarbonate) the reaction is called **thermal decomposition**.

> **Exam tip**
>
> It is important that you do not mix up the effects of acid and heat on sodium hydrogencarbonate.

Baking powder

Baking powder contains sodium hydrogencarbonate and tartaric acid. Baking powder is a solid and is sold in packets or small containers. It is used in baking to help the bread or cake mixture to rise, which gives it a lighter texture and makes the product less dense.

Tartaric acid provides acidity, so neutralisation takes place and carbon dioxide is produced.

The word equation for using baking soda and tartaric acid in baking is:

> **Exam tip**
>
> The use of tartaric acid benefits the baking process because it means there are two different reactions producing carbon dioxide.

sodium hydrogencarbonate + tartaric acid → sodium tartrate + carbon dioxide + water

Sherbet

Sherbet is a mixture of sodium hydrogencarbonate, sugar and solid citric acid. When water is added, the sodium hydrogencarbonate and citric acid react (another neutralisation reaction). This is what happens when you eat sherbet – the water (saliva) in your mouth causes the reaction. The carbon dioxide gas produced causes a fizzing sensation.

The word equation to describe how sherbet produces this fizzing feeling is:

> **Exam tip**
>
> It is important to use a weak acid such as tartaric acid in baking soda. A strong acid would produce carbon dioxide too quickly and it would not form the light texture typical of bread and cakes. It would also leave the bread and cakes too acidic to eat.

sodium hydrogencarbonate + citric acid → sodium citrate + carbon dioxide + water

1 The table gives information about two different indicators.

Substance	Red cabbage dye	Universal indicator	pH range
water	purple	green	7
sodium hydroxide	yellow	dark blue	12–14
hydrochloric acid	red	red	1–2
vinegar	red	orange	3–4

a) Suggest what colour red cabbage dye will be if it is added to nitric acid. [1]

b) Use the table to explain fully why universal indicator is a more effective indicator than red cabbage. [2]

c) Explain how red cabbage indicator can be made. [3]   **[6 marks]**

2 The pH changes when hydrochloric acid is added to sodium hydroxide are shown in the graph.

a) What was the pH value of the sodium hydroxide solution at the start of the investigation? [1]

b) Name the type of reaction involved. [1]

c) Suggest why a pH sensor was used in this investigation. [1]

d) Name a suitable piece of apparatus that could have been used to add the hydrochloric acid. [1]

[4 marks]

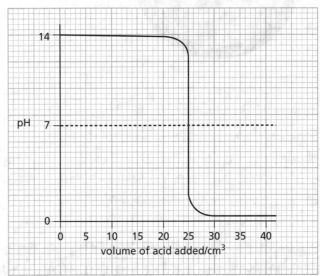

3 The chemical formula for sulfuric acid is H_2SO_4.

a) How many elements are present in sulfuric acid? [1]

b) How many atoms does this formula represent? [1]   **[2 marks]**

4 a) Describe what causes indigestion. [1]

b) Explain how sodium hydrogencarbonate can cure indigestion. [3]

c) Explain why indigestion remedies can cause people to suffer 'wind'. [1]   **[5 marks]**

5 Sherbet reacts with water in the mouth to produce a fizzing sensation.

a) Copy and complete the word equation for this reaction:

sodium hydrogencarbonate + citric acid → _____ + _____ + _____ [3]

b) Explain what causes the fizzing sensation. [1]   **[4 marks]**

6 This word equation shows sodium hydroxide reacting with sulfuric acid:

sodium hydroxide + sulfuric acid → sodium sulfate + water

a) Name the salt made in this reaction. [1]

b) Balance the symbol equation: [2]   **[3 marks]**

$NaOH + H_2SO_4 \rightarrow Na_2SO_4 + H_2O$

8 The world about us

The structure of the Earth

Figure 8.1 shows the structure of the Earth.

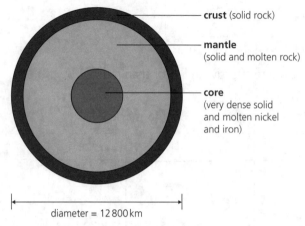

crust (solid rock)

mantle
(solid and molten rock)

core
(very dense solid
and molten nickel
and iron)

diameter = 12 800 km

↑ Figure 8.1 The structure of the Earth

Some key points about the structure of the Earth:

● the Earth gets hotter, the closer to the core – the core is hotter than the mantle, and the mantle is hotter than the crust

● the crust is a solid layer of uneven thickness – it is thicker in mountainous zones and thinner under deep oceans.

Tectonic plates, volcanoes and earthquakes

The theory of plate tectonics helps to explain what causes earthquakes, and why volcanoes and the building of mountains occur.

Plate tectonics

The Earth's crust is made up of massive **tectonic plates** that float on the mantle. This happens because the crust is less dense than the mantle. The movement of molten rock in the mantle causes the tectonic plates in the crust to move slowly. Figure 8.2 shows the tectonic plates in the crust and their main directions of movement.

> **Exam tip**
>
> You do not need to remember Figure 8.2. However, you should understand that tectonic plates are very large, and that volcanoes and earthquakes are more likely to occur at their edges (see later).

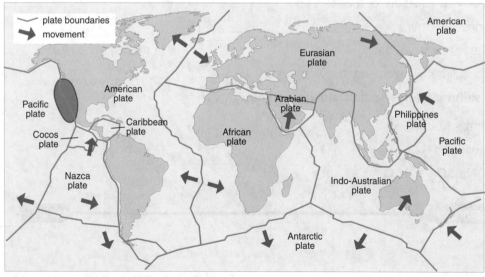

↑ Figure 8.2 Tectonic plates in the Earth's crust

Wegener's theory of continental drift

Alfred Wegener (a German scientist) proposed the theory of **continental drift** in 1912. Wegener suggested that the continents on the surface of the Earth are moving. He proposed that millions of years ago, the land on the Earth was one large mass and since then large sections (the continents) have split from each other and drifted apart.

Wegener used several lines of evidence to support his theory:

● The shape of the continents – Figure 8.3 shows how neatly east South America and west Africa join together like jigsaw pieces. This can be explained by the continents once being linked and then separating. Other continents fit neatly together in the same way.

● The rock types, animals and fossils found in different continents match as if the continents had been joined.

Figure 8.3 summarises the evidence Wegener used to support his theory.

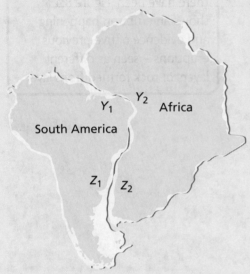

rock types, living organisms and fossils are very similar at Y_1 and Y_2 and also at Z_1 and Z_2 they are much less similar between Y and Z, because they were originally much further apart

↑ Figure 8.3 Evidence for Wegener's theory

Exam tip

It is important to note that although Wegener's evidence of continental drift was very strong, he could not explain the process of continental drift. People were not aware of plate tectonics – the theory that could explain continental drift – until the 1950s. This is the main reason why there was much opposition to his theory.

Many people rejected Wegener's theory of continental drift because:

● they could not see it happening – the rate of movement is extremely slow

● there was no explanation for continental drift.

Earthquakes

An **earthquake** is caused by the edges of two tectonic plates moving against/alongside/over each other at plate boundaries. Most earthquakes happen over a very short time. However, the earthquake usually follows a longer period of tension as forces build up in the plates before suddenly moving with a massive release of energy.

There are some key points about earthquakes:

● the strength of an earthquake is measured using the **Richter scale** **0** (very weak) → (very powerful) **10**

● the strength and duration of an earthquake can be measured on graphs called **seismographs**

● scientists cannot accurately predict when an earthquake will occur

● most people killed by earthquakes are killed by falling buildings or man-made structures such as bridges.

Exam tip

Have another look at Figure 8.2. You should be able to explain why an earthquake is more likely in western California (the area shaded red) rather than in Britain.

Volcanoes

Volcanoes also occur at the edges of tectonic plates. They usually occur when tectonic plates are being pulled apart (or even pushed together). This allows molten **magma** in the mantle to reach the surface. The magma comes up through vents in the volcano and comes out of the crater. The molten rock flowing down the sides of the volcano is called **lava**.

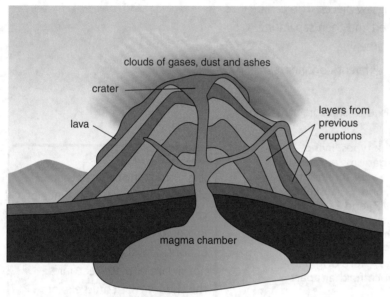

↑ **Figure 8.4 The structure of a volcano**

Exam tip

In an exam you may be asked to label diagrams of volcanoes and state how many eruptions there have been. Figure 8.4 shows an eruption happening and evidence of five previous eruptions – seen as different layers of rock formed from lava.

Volcanoes can remain dormant (not erupting) for very long periods and then suddenly **erupt** with great force. As well as producing lava (which can flow well beyond the rim of the volcano causing great destruction), dust and ashes can be forced high into the atmosphere. As with earthquakes, it is very difficult to predict when a volcano will erupt.

Worked example

a) Describe the process of a volcanic eruption.

b) Suggest why many people are killed by some volcanic eruptions.

Answer

a) Gaps/weakness appear in the Earth's crust. Molten magma flows up through vents in the volcano. Lava flows down the sides of the volcano and turns into rock.

b) Eruptions are unpredictable with no warning. Living things are killed by hot lava flowing across the land.

Mountain building

The movement of tectonic plates also leads to mountain building over very long periods of time. If two tectonic plates are moving towards each other, their edges will collide and the forces will push the edges upwards to form mountains. The leading edge of one tectonic plate can also move under the edge of another forcing it up. This is why mountain ranges are commonly found near the boundaries of tectonic plates.

There are three main different types of rock found on the Earth's surface – **sedimentary**, **igneous** and **metamorphic**. Features of these rocks are described in the table.

Rock type	How formed	Example
igneous	formed by volcanic activity – igneous rocks form as lava cools	granite basalt
sedimentary	formed by small rock particles (e.g. grit) and the remains of dead plants and animals forming layers of sediment on the Earth's surface – these layers are compressed by the weight of more sediment deposited above them over millions of years	limestone sandstone
metamorphic	the effect of heat and/or pressure can change already formed igneous or sedimentary rocks into metamorphic rocks – for example, the rocks on either side of a volcanic vent are likely to be metamorphosed	marble slate

Fossils

Fossils are the remains of dead plants and animals preserved in sedimentary rock. The plants and animals were buried in the sediment that the sedimentary rocks were formed from. The pressure from the layers above preserved the fossils in their original shape and size (similar to a flower-press preserving flowers).

Most fossils have been found on (or close to) the Earth's surface. This shows that there have been great changes to the Earth's surface over time. For example, the relative positions of layers of rock have changed due to forces acting within the Earth's crust. Also, the action of the weather has caused the upper layers of rocks to be worn away (weathered) to expose fossils.

The age of the Earth   Revised

There are a number of ways in which the age of the Earth can be estimated.

Archbishop Ussher's method

In 1648 Archbishop Ussher used the Book of Genesis in the Bible to calculate the age of the Earth. He calculated the number of generations (you and your siblings/friends are one generation; your parents are the previous generation; your grandparents an earlier generation; and so on) there have been, starting with Adam and Eve.

Ussher's conclusions were that the Earth was created in 4004 BC, meaning that the Earth is around 6000 years old.

Radiometric dating

Many **igneous rocks** contain radioactive isotopes of elements such as potassium. These **radioactive isotopes** decay and breakdown at a constant rate over a period of time. The process of **radiometric dating** compares the proportions of parent (undecayed) isotopes and decayed daughter nuclei. Knowing the rate of decay for a particular isotope allows scientists to estimate the age of rocks very accurately.

Using radiometric dating (and other modern scientific evidence) the actual age of the Earth is around 4.5 billion (4 500 000 000 or 4500 million) years.

Scientists refer to the idea of '**deep time**'. This term is used to help in explaining the idea that the timescales involved in the development of the Earth are beyond most people's comprehension. It is very hard to imagine a time period of 4.5 billion years!

Revision questions
Tested

1 The diagram below shows the movement of a number of tectonic plates.

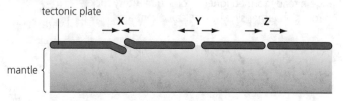

tectonic plate

X   Y   Z

mantle

a) What is meant by the theory of plate tectonics? [2]

b) Use the letters **X**, **Y** and **Z** to suggest where:

   i) a volcano is most likely to occur [1]

   ii) mountains are most likely to form. [1]

c) Describe how earthquakes occur. [1]

d) Name the scale used to measure the intensity of an earthquake. [1]   **[6 marks]**

2 a) Describe Wegener's theory of continental drift. [3]

   b) State two pieces of evidence that can be used to support his theory. [2]   **[5 marks]**

3 a) Describe how sedimentary rocks are formed. [3]

   b) Name two sedimentary rocks. [2]   **[5 marks]**

4 Describe the process of radiometric dating.   **[3 marks]**

Go online for the answers
Online

9 Elements and compounds

Atoms

An **element** is a pure chemical substance that is made from only one type of **atom**. An element cannot be chemically broken down into anything simpler.

It was once thought that atoms were the smallest unit of matter. We now know that atoms are made up of three **subatomic** particles – **protons**, **electrons** and **neutrons**.

The protons and neutrons are found in a central **nucleus**. The electrons are arranged in **shells** that surround the nucleus.

Some properties of atoms:

● **Mass** – protons and neutrons have the same mass. However, the mass of an electron is negligible (relative to the mass of a proton and a neutron).

● **Charge** – protons have a positive charge and electrons have a negative charge; neutrons have no charge. In atoms, the numbers of protons and electrons are equal – this means that an atom is electrically neutral and has no charge.

This table summarises the properties of atoms.

Subatomic particle	Relative mass	Relative charge
proton	1	+1
neutron	1	0
electron	$\frac{1}{1840}$ (negligible)	−1

nucleus containing protons and neutrons

shells containing moving electrons

↑ **Figure 9.1 The structure of an atom**

Exam tip

The information in this table is frequently asked in examinations – it is important that you learn it.

Atomic number and mass number

Atomic number – all atoms have an atomic number. This is the number of protons in the nucleus. This is the same as the number of electrons orbiting the nucleus.

Mass number – all atoms also have a mass number. This is the total number of protons and neutrons in the nucleus. Because the mass of a proton is 1 unit and the mass of a neutron is 1 unit, the mass number = the number of protons + the number of neutrons.

The Periodic Table gives the atomic number and mass number of each element. For example, oxygen has an atomic number of 8 and a mass number of 16. Figure 9.2 shows how oxygen is represented in the Periodic Table.

We can use the information in Figure 9.2 to work out the number of each of the subatomic particles in an atom of oxygen:

● the atomic number = the number of protons

● the mass number = the number of protons + the number of neutrons

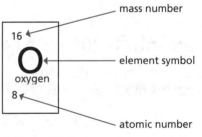

mass number

element symbol

atomic number

↑ **Figure 9.2 Oxygen atom description**

Also, oxygen atoms must have 8 electrons because the number of electrons = the number of protons. They must have 8 neutrons because the number of neutrons = the mass number − the number of protons.

Worked example

An atom of potassium is represented as $^{39}_{19}K$.

a) Calculate the number of electrons in an atom of potassium.

b) Calculate the number of neutrons in an atom of potassium.

Answer

a) 19 is the atomic number, which is the number of protons – so there must be 19 electrons.

b) 39 is the mass number and the number of neutrons = mass number − atomic number = 39 − 19 = 20

Electron arrangement (electronic structure)

The electrons in an atom orbit (or travel) around the nucleus in 'shells'. The first shell (the one closest to the nucleus) can have a maximum of two electrons in it. The second and third shells can hold a maximum of eight electrons. The shells fill up in order – so if an atom has six electrons, it will have two in the first shell and four in the second shell.

Figure 9.3 shows the electron arrangement (configuration) of a sodium atom to be 2, 8, 1 – this means there are two electrons in the first shell, eight in the second and one in the third.

Exam tip

You need to be able to work out electron arrangements from atomic numbers. For sodium, the atomic number is 11 – so there are 11 electrons in its atoms. Remember that they fill up the shells in turn. The first shell has the maximum 2; the second shell the maximum 8; and there is 1 electron in the third shell.

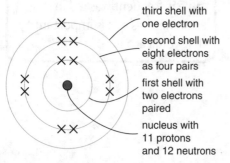

third shell with one electron

second shell with eight electrons as four pairs

first shell with two electrons paired

nucleus with 11 protons and 12 neutrons

↑ **Figure 9.3 The arrangement of electrons in a sodium atom**

Elements 1–20

Figure 9.4 on the next page shows the electronic structure for atoms of elements with atomic numbers 1 to 20.

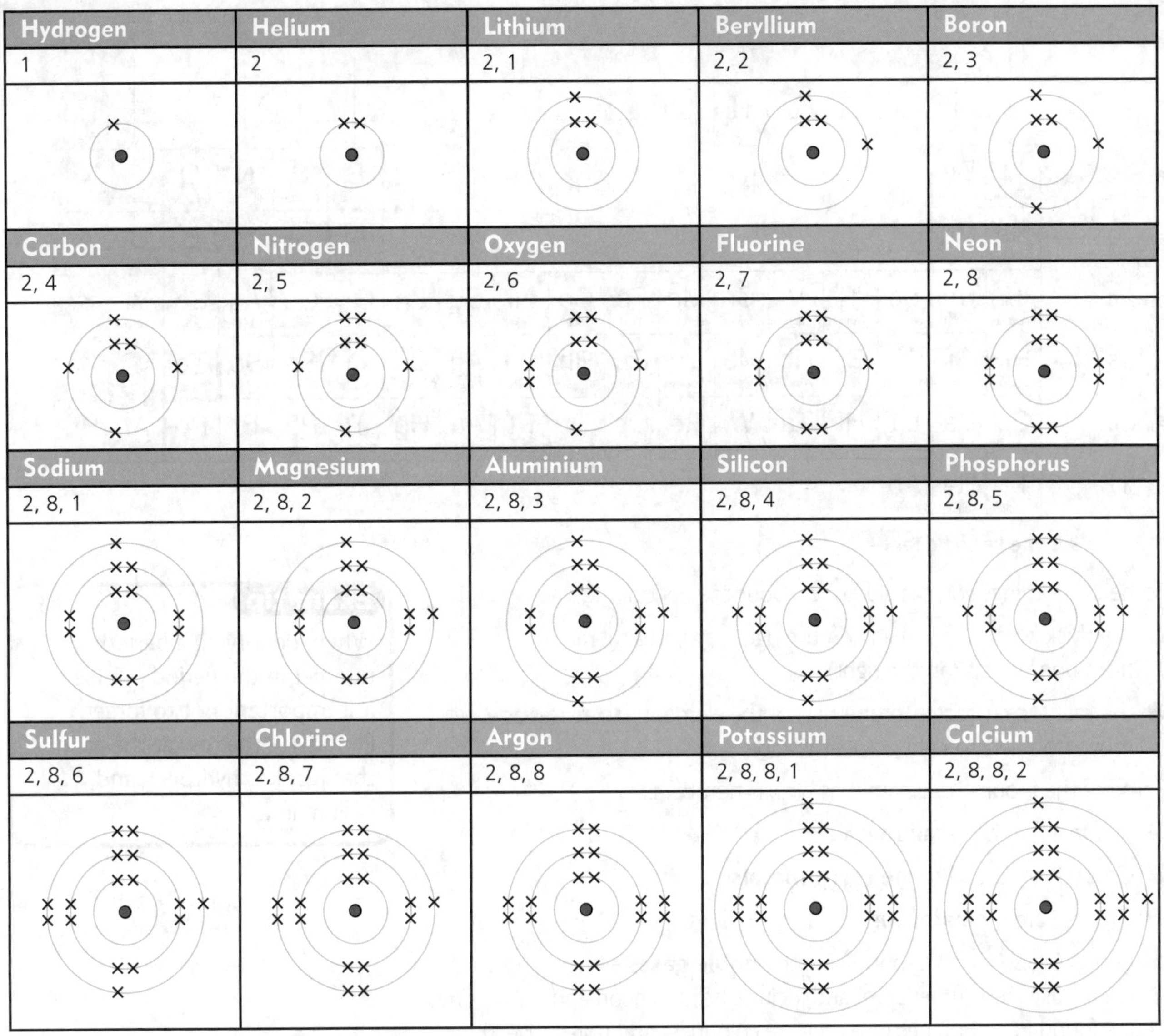

Hydrogen	Helium	Lithium	Beryllium	Boron
1	2	2, 1	2, 2	2, 3
Carbon	Nitrogen	Oxygen	Fluorine	Neon
2, 4	2, 5	2, 6	2, 7	2, 8
Sodium	Magnesium	Aluminium	Silicon	Phosphorus
2, 8, 1	2, 8, 2	2, 8, 3	2, 8, 4	2, 8, 5
Sulfur	Chlorine	Argon	Potassium	Calcium
2, 8, 6	2, 8, 7	2, 8, 8	2, 8, 8, 1	2, 8, 8, 2

↑ Figure 9.4 The arrangement of electrons in atoms of elements 1–20. Note that hydrogen, with atomic number 1, has 1 electron; helium, with atomic number 2, has 2 electrons and so on until calcium, which has 20 electrons.

Following the rules of electron shells filling in order, calcium has an electronic structure of 2, 8, 8, 2 with the first three shells filled.

The Periodic Table

Revised

The Periodic Table lists all the known elements – they are arranged in an order based on their atomic numbers.

In the Periodic Table:

● the horizontal rows are called **periods**

● the vertical columns are called **groups** – the elements in each group have similar properties.

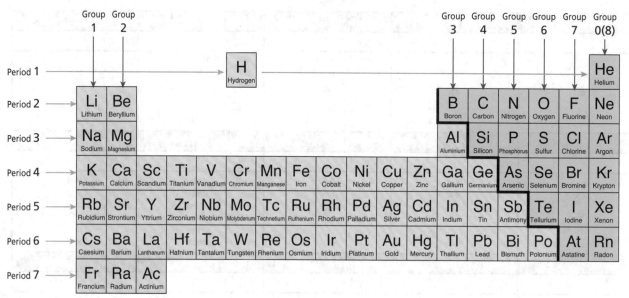

↑ **Figure 9.5 The Periodic Table**

Some other things you should know about the Periodic Table:

- the thick black stepped line on the right separates metals (on the left) from non-metals (on the right)
- the metallic character (properties) of the elements decreases as you move from left to right across the table.

Some of the groups have names as well as numbers:

- Group 1 are the **alkali metals**
- Group 2 are the **alkaline earth metals**
- Group 7 are the **halogens**
- Group 0 (also called Group 8) are the **noble gases** – these gases are chemically inert (unreactive) and include helium, neon and argon. They are found in air but, because they are colourless and unreactive, they were discovered much later than many other elements.

Exam tip

When identifying a period number in the Periodic Table, it is important not to forget Period 1 – the row at the top that just has hydrogen and helium in it.

Periods and groups

In the Periodic Table the **period (row) number** gives the number of **electron shells** in each atom.

The **group (column) number** gives the number of **electrons** in the **outer shell** of the atoms.

For example, sodium (Na) is in Period 3 and Group 1. This means it has three electron shells and only one electron in the outer shell. With the inner shells needing to be filled before outer shells are used, the electron arrangement for sodium is 2, 8, 1.

Worked example

What is the electronic structure of a sulfur atom?

Answer

Use the Periodic Table to identify that sulfur is in Period 3 and Group 6 – and has an atomic number 16.

This means it has three shells and six electrons in the outer (third) shell.

The electronic structure of sulfur is therefre 2, 8, 6.

Compounds and naming them

A compound is a substance that has two or more elements chemically joined together. Compounds are formed when two atoms share electrons or when electrons move from one atom to another.

When a compound is formed between a metal and a non-metal, the metal element (or the element to the left/lower down) keeps its name. The other element in the compound changes its name.

● sodium and fluorine combine to form sodium fluor**ide** – NaF

● the same rule applies for simple compounds formed from non-metals – for example hydrogen (to the left of chlorine) and chlorine form hydrogen chlor**ide**.

Generally, you should be aware that substances with names ending in **–ide** have two elements and those ending in **–ate** have three elements, one of which is oxygen. For example, sodium fluor**ide** (NaF) is formed from sodium and fluorine; magnesium sulf**ate** ($MgSO_4$) is formed from magnesium, sulfur and oxygen. There is an exception to the –ide rule – hydroxides have three elements For example potassium hydroxide (KOH) is formed from potassium, hydrogen and oxygen.

Some compounds, such as methane (CH_4), have only one name. Sometimes a molecule is formed from two identical atoms (from the same element) joined together – like oxygen (O_2) and hydrogen (H_2).

The alkali metals (Group 1)

The alkali metals are so reactive that they need to be stored under oil to stop them reacting with air. They are soft grey metals that can be easily cut with a knife.

They all react with water. If **lithium** is added to water it moves around vigorously on the surface (floats) and makes a hissing sound as hydrogen gas is produced. It dissolves and disappears as it is used up in the reaction. The word equation for lithium reacting with water is:

lithium + water → lithium hydroxide + hydrogen

As you move down Group 1 in the Periodic Table the reaction of the metal with water becomes increasingly vigorous. This is because the metals are more reactive as you move down the table.

All the Group 1 (alkali) metals react with water to form a metal hydroxide and release hydrogen gas. In effect:

alkali metal + water → metal hydroxide + hydrogen

Worked example

a) Explain why the alkali metals are stored in oil and not water.

b) Write the word equation for sodium reacting with water.

Answer

a) They all react with water / they are unreactive in oil / stops reaction with air

b) sodium + water → sodium hydroxide + hydrogen

> **Exam tip**
>
> You should remember that the reactions between Group 1 metals and water get more vigorous in the sequence lithium < sodium < potassium < rubidium < caesium < francium (i.e. moving down the group).

The balanced symbol equations for the reactions of lithium and sodium with water are:

$$2Li + 2H_2O \rightarrow 2LiOH + H_2$$
$$2Na + 2H_2O \rightarrow 2NaOH + H_2$$

The other reactions between alkali metals and water are balanced in the same way.

Other metals
Revised

The other metals in the Periodic Table are less reactive than the alkali metals. They include magnesium, zinc, iron and copper. Because they are less reactive, they will react only slowly with water, but most of these metals will react with dilute acids (e.g. hydrochloric acid).

When these metals react with acid, a salt and hydrogen are produced:

metal + acid → salt + hydrogen

For example:

magnesium + hydrochloric acid → magnesium chloride + hydrogen

zinc + sulfuric acid → zinc sulfate + hydrogen

The balanced symbol equations for these reactions are:

$$Mg + 2HCl \rightarrow MgCl_2 + H_2$$
$$Zn + H_2SO_4 \rightarrow ZnSO_4 + H_2$$

The order of reactivity – the reactivity series

Although both zinc and magnesium react with acid, they are not equally reactive – magnesium is more reactive. However, copper is not reactive at all – it will not react with dilute acid. Iron is slightly reactive, but not as reactive as zinc.

Based on the rate of production of hydrogen bubbles when the metals in this section are added to a dilute acid, the order of reactivity (or **reactivity series**) is:

[most reactive] **magnesium > zinc > iron > copper** [least reactive]

Displacement reactions

When a metal compound is dissolved in water and another metal added, a **displacement reaction** can occur. However, displacement reactions only happen if the metal being added is more reactive than the metal in the dissolved compound.

Figure 9.6 shows what happens when an iron nail is stood in a solution of copper(II) sulfate.

Iron is more reactive than copper (see the reactivity series above) so the iron displaces the copper from the solution to form iron sulfate. The (displaced) copper forms a coat (layer) on the iron nail.

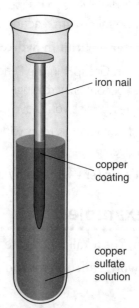

iron nail

copper coating

copper sulfate solution

↑ Figure 9.6 A displacement reaction with iron and copper sulfate solution

The word equation for this reaction is:

iron + copper(II) sulfate → copper + iron(II) sulphate

The balanced symbol equation for this reaction is:

Fe + CuSO$_4$ → Cu + FeSO$_4$

Displacement reactions can be used to determine a reactivity series in a similar way to the rate of production of hydrogen bubbles when the metals reacted with dilute acid.

This is done by putting metals into metal salt solutions of the other metals in the series. For example, magnesium with copper(II) sulfate, iron(II) sulfate and zinc sulfate. This is repeated using zinc with copper(II) sulfate, iron(II) sulfate and magnesium sulphate.

The results are shown in the following table.

	magnesium sulfate	zinc sulfate	iron(II) sulfate	copper(II) sulfate
magnesium		displacement reaction	displacement reaction	displacement reaction
zinc	no reaction		displacement reaction	displacement reaction
iron	no reaction	no reaction		displacement reaction
copper	no reaction	no reaction	no reaction	

These results show that magnesium is the most reactive metal because it displaces the other three metals from solutions of their salts. Copper does not displace any of the other metals, so it is the least reactive. Zinc displaces both iron and copper, and iron displaces copper only.

The reactivity series based on displacement reactions is:

[most reactive] **magnesium > zinc > iron > copper** [least reactive]

The word equations follow the same format as for iron displacing the copper when the iron was mixed with copper(II) sulfate solution. For example, when magnesium is added to zinc sulfate the reaction is:

magnesium + zinc sulfate → magnesium sulfate + zinc

The balanced symbol equation for this reaction is:

Mg + ZnSO$_4$ → MgSO$_4$ + Zn

History of the Periodic Table
Revised

The ancient **Greeks** believed that everything was made up of four different elements – **earth**, **air**, **fire** and **water**.

In 1864 **John Newlands** arranged the elements (that were known at that time) in order of atomic weight (atomic number). He found similarities in every eighth element. For example, the first element was similar to the eighth, the second to the ninth, the third to the tenth and so on. This pattern was called Newlands' **law of octaves**.

Newlands used other observations such as colour and reactivity as well as atomic weight to put the elements in order.

There were problems with Newlands' law of octaves. Some elements did not fit the pattern, the noble gases had not been discovered and he did not take account of yet-to-be-discovered elements.

Dmitri Mendeleev (1869) was able to improve on Newlands' model. Mendeleev also arranged the elements in order of atomic weight but he left gaps for yet-to-be-discovered elements – having done this he was brave enough to predict the properties of these undiscovered elements.

The **modern Periodic Table** is very similar to Mendeleev's. However, with the new-found knowledge of atomic structure, it is arranged so that the group number gives the number of electrons in the outer shell, and the period number gives the number of electron shells.

Ionic and covalent compounds

Revised

Compounds formed from metal elements and non-metal elements are **ionic** compounds. In making these compounds, electrons are transferred from one atom to another. Compounds that are made from only non-metal elements are called **covalent** compounds.

Ionic compounds

Examples include sodium (metal) chloride (non-metal) and magnesium (metal) oxide (non-metal). Ionic compounds are made up of charged particles called **ions**. Ionic compounds contain positive ions and negative ions – for example Na^+ (positive because an electron was lost from a sodium atom) and Cl^- (negative because an electron was gained by a chlorine atom).

When forming an ionic compound, a transfer of electrons occurs. The metal atoms lose electrons and give them to the non-metal atoms. Each atom gives or loses enough electrons to form full outer shells for both ions.

Examples of ionic bonding can be seen in combinations involving:

● Group 1 (alkali) metals with Group 7 (halogens) non-metals – e.g. NaCl

● Group 2 (alkaline earth) metals with Group 6 non-metals – e.g. MgO

Sodium chloride (NaCl) When sodium (electronic configuration 2, 8, 1) reacts with chlorine (electronic configuration 2, 8, 7), the single electron in sodium's third shell is **transferred** to the outer (third) shell of the chlorine.

The sodium has lost an electron so is no longer electrically neutral – it has 11 protons and now only 10 electrons (it lost an electron) so is represented by Na^+. The chlorine, having gained one electron has 18 electrons (but still 17 protons in the nucleus) so is electrically negative and is represented by Cl^-.

Because the Na^+ and the Cl^- are electrically opposite, they are attracted to each other to form the ionic compound sodium chloride – note that the ions are not called 'chlorine' ions but chloride ions.

In the resulting compound, sodium chloride, both the sodium ions and the chloride ions now have full outer shells (sodium 2 , 8 and chloride 2, 8, 8).

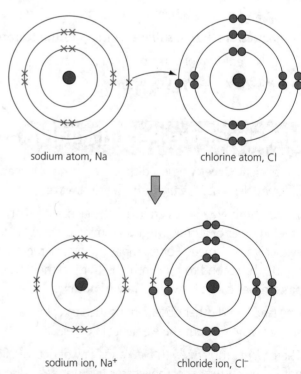

sodium atom, Na   chlorine atom, Cl

sodium ion, Na^+ chloride ion, Cl^-

↑ **Figure 9.7 Ion formation in sodium chloride**

Worked example

Describe the ionic bonding in the formation of magnesium oxide.

Answer

A magnesium atom has electronic configuration 2, 8, 2 and an oxygen atom 2, 6

Two electrons are transferred from the magnesium (metal) atoms to the oxygen (non-metal) atoms to make both outer shells full – magnesium with 2, 8; oxide with 2, 8

The magnesium ion is Mg^{2+} and the oxide ion is O^{2-}

The oppositely charged ions are attracted to each other and form the ionic compound magnesium oxide – MgO. This is electrically neutral because the positive ion charges and the negative ion charges cancel each other out.

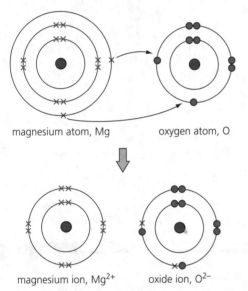

magnesium atom, Mg   oxygen atom, O

magnesium ion, Mg^{2+} oxide ion, O^{2-}

↑ **Figure 9.8 Ion formation in magnesium oxide**

Exam tip

'Mg^{2+}' means that the magnesium ions have two fewer electrons than protons; 'O^{2-}' means that the oxide ions have two more electrons than protons.

Covalent compounds

When non-metal atoms bond to form molecules, they **share** electrons (rather than transferring them from one atom to the other). This is to give every atom in the final molecule a full outer shell. The shared electrons count in the electronic configuration of both atoms. The shared electrons make a **covalent bond** that holds the atoms together.

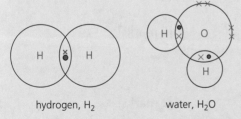

hydrogen, H_2 water, H_2O

Figure 9.9 Covalent bonding in hydrogen (H_2) and water (H_2O)

Oxidation and reduction

Oxidation happens when a reactant gains oxygen. **Reduction** happens when a reactant loses oxygen.

Oxidation

When magnesium burns in air, it gains oxygen to form magnesium oxide. This is an example of an oxidation reaction – any reaction that involves a gain of oxygen is oxidation.

The word equation for the oxidation of magnesium is:

magnesium + oxygen → magnesium oxide

The balanced symbol equation is:

$2Mg + O_2 → 2MgO$

Reduction

Copper oxide reacts with hydrogen to form copper and water. In this reaction the copper loses oxygen to form water – the copper oxide is reduced because it loses oxygen; the hydrogen is oxidised to form water.

The word equation for the reduction of copper oxide is:

copper oxide + hydrogen → copper + water

The balanced symbol equation is:

$CuO + H_2 → Cu + H_2O$

Revision questions

1 The diagram shows the structure of an atom.

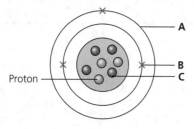

Proton

a) Name the parts labelled **A**, **B** and **C**. [3]

b) Give the atomic number of this atom. [1]

c) Give the mass number of this atom. [1]

d) Give the electronic structure of this atom. [1]   **[6 marks]**

2 $NaNO_3$ is sodium nitrate.

a) How many elements are in sodium nitrate? [1]

b) How many atoms does this formula represent? [1]   **[2 marks]**

3 Write the balanced symbol equation for the reaction between potassium (an alkali metal) and water.   **[3 marks]**

4 The table below compares the reactivity of three metals (magnesium, copper and zinc) by adding a small amount of each to sulfate solutions of the other metals.

	magnesium sulfate	copper(II) sulfate	zinc sulfate
magnesium		reaction	reaction
copper	no reaction		no reaction
zinc	no reaction	reaction	

a) Which metal is most reactive? [1]

b) Complete a reactivity series for the three metals. [1]

c) Copy and complete the word equation for the reaction of magnesium with copper sulfate: [2]

magnesium + copper(II) sulfate → _____ + _____

d) What name is given to this type of reaction? [1]

e) Describe and explain one observation you would see when magnesium is added to the copper(II) sulfate solution. [2]   **[7 marks]**

5 Shown below is an outline of the Periodic Table.

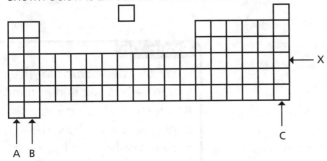

A B

C

X

a) What do the small square boxes represent? [1]

b) Name the groups labelled **A**, **B** and **C**. [3]

c) Identify the number of period **X**. [1]

d) How many electrons are in the outer shell of an atom of a Group **B** element? [1]   **[6 marks]**

6 Explain, in terms of ion formation, how sodium chloride is formed from sodium and chlorine.   **[5 marks]**

Go online for the answers   Online

10 Oil, polymers and materials

Fossil fuels
Revised

Fossil fuels include **coal**, **oil** and **gas**.

Coal is made from plants that died millions of years ago. Over this time, pressure and heat have turned the remains of the dead plants into coal.

Coal is mainly formed of the element carbon. When coal (or any other fossil fuel) burns it reacts with oxygen (in the air) producing oxides. The burning of a fuel is called **combustion** and heat is released as a by-product. The word equation for the combustion of coal is:

carbon + oxygen → carbon dioxide (+ heat)

The balanced symbol equation for the combustion of coal is:

$$C + O_2 \rightarrow CO_2$$

Crude oil
Revised

Crude oil is also a fossil fuel formed from plants and animals that died millions of years ago. Pressure and heat changed their remains into crude oil. It is a liquid mixture containing hundreds of different substances. As well as liquids, crude oil contains some gases and dissolved solids.

Hydrocarbons

The substances in crude oil are **hydrocarbons** – these are compounds containing carbon and hydrogen only.

For example, two hydrocarbons present in crude oil are ethane (C_2H_6) and propane (C_3H_8).

> **Exam tip**
>
> If you are asked to explain what a hydrocarbon is, it is important to state that a hydrocarbon is a compound containing the elements carbon and hydrogen **only** – many other substances contain carbon and hydrogen, but other elements as well.

Separating crude oil (fractional distillation)

Because crude oil is a mixture of different substances, the different compounds can be separated by **fractional distillation** – this process involves:

● Heating the crude oil.

● It evaporates causing most of the oil to become a mixture of gases.

● The gases move up the fractioning column (steel tower) used for fractional distillation.

● The original **liquid hydrocarbons** condense back into a liquid – this happens as they cool to their boiling point.

● Because the tower is cooler at the top than the bottom, different liquids condense at different levels in the tower – the liquids are collected separately.

● The **solids** dissolved in crude oil (tar/bitumen) drain out the bottom of the tower (they did not evaporate).

● The **gases** do not condense – they come out of the top of the tower as refinery gases.

> **Exam tip**
>
> 'Condense' is a term meaning 'change from a gas to a liquid'. For example, water vapour condenses into liquid water as it cools. This change takes place at the boiling point of the substance.

There are three key points about the fractional distillation of crude oil:

● The different components produced are called **fractions**.

● All the fractions are **hydrocarbons**.

● Each fraction (separated at a particular position in the tower) has a similar number of carbon atoms – the smaller hydrocarbons with smaller numbers of carbon atoms in their molecules form the fractions at the top of the tower.

Figure 10.1 shows the fractional distillation of crude oil, the products obtained and their main uses.

Exam tip

The term 'fractional distillation' summarises what happens. Distillation involves heating liquids causing them to evaporate into gas and then condensing them back into liquids as they reach a cooler zone. 'Fractional' means that this happens to the different substances in different places because they have **different boiling points**.

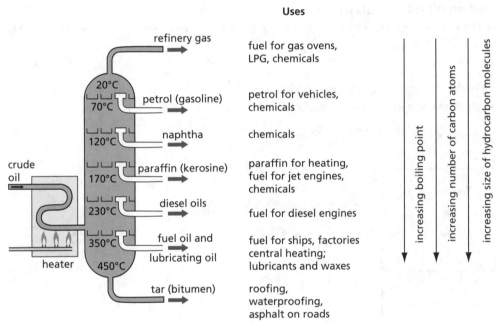

↑ **Figure 10.1 The fractional distillation of crude oil**

Finding and using crude oil

Crude oil is a finite resource – this means that it is **non-renewable** and that there is a limited supply. Scientists have taken three main approaches to solving this problem:

● Using **alternative (renewable) fuels** – there is an increased emphasis on using renewable energy, such as that generated by wind turbines or hydroelectric power.

● More efficient **recycling** of products made from oil – e.g. plastics.

● Better or different methods for finding and extracting gas and oil – e.g. fracking.

Exam tip

You need to know the uses of the different fractions of crude oil as shown in Figure 10.1. You also need to appreciate that the fractions closer to the *top* of the tower condense at lower temperatures than the fractions *lower* down.

The combustion of hydrocarbons

All hydrocarbons can be burned – some more easily than others. When hydrocarbon fuels are combusted in air, the hydrogen reacts with the oxygen to form water, and the carbon reacts with the oxygen to form carbon dioxide – combustion also releases heat energy, although this is not shown in equations:

hydrocarbon + oxygen → carbon dioxide + water

For example:

butane + oxygen → carbon dioxide + water

Worked example
Write a word equation for the combustion of methane (natural gas).

Answer

methane + oxygen → carbon dioxide + water

The alkanes

Alkanes are a unique group of hydrocarbons – they include methane, ethane, propane and butane, which are all gases found in crude oil.

In the alkanes, each molecule has carbon atoms with four bonds as shown in Figure 10.2.

Name	Molecular formula	Structural formula
methane	CH_4	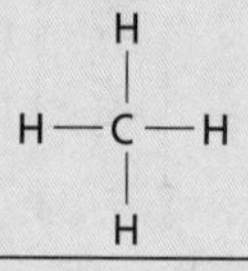 H | H — C — H | H
ethane	C_2H_6	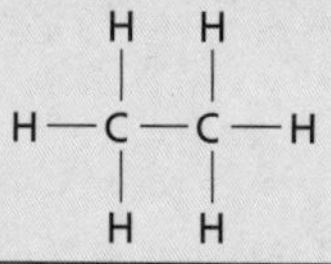 H H | | H — C — C — H | | H H
propane	C_3H_8	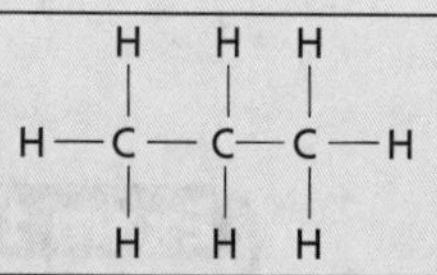 H H H | | | H — C — C — C — H | | | H H H
butane	C_4H_{10}	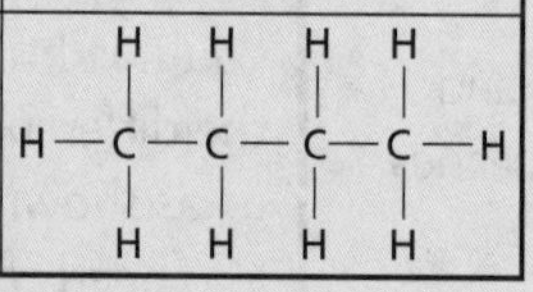 H H H H | | | | H — C — C — C — C — H | | | | H H H H

← Figure 10.2 The first four alkanes

You should be able to write balanced symbol equations for combustion. Taking methane as an example – start with the word equation for the reaction:

methane + oxygen → carbon dioxide + water

Then do the balancing as follows:

$CH_4 + O_2 \rightarrow CO_2 + H_2O$ (symbol equation before balancing)

$CH_4 + 2O_2 \rightarrow CO_2 + 2H_2O$ (balanced symbol equation)

The equation had to be balanced by writing '2' in front of 'O_2' and '2' in front of 'H_2O' – to get four O atoms and four H atoms on both sides of the equation.

> **Exam tip**
>
> If you are asked to draw any of the alkanes in Figure 10.2, you can check that you are correct by making sure the numbers of carbon atoms and hydrogen atoms match the molecular formula, and also that all the carbon atom have four bonds.

Worked example

Write a balanced symbol equation showing the complete combustion of propane.

Answer

propane + oxygen → carbon dioxide + water (word equation)

C_3H_8 + O_2 → CO_2 + H_2O (symbol equation before balancing)

There are three C atoms in C_3H_8 (left-hand side) so '3' is the balancing number in front of CO_2 (right-hand side). So:

C_3H_8 + O_2 → $3CO_2$ + H_2O

There are eight H atoms in C_3H_8 so '4' is the balancing number in front of H_2O to give eight hydrogen atom on both sides.

The next step is to balance the oxygen atoms:

C_3H_8 + O_2 → $3CO_2$ + $4H_2O$

There are six O atoms in $3CO_2$ and four in $4H_2O$ – a total of ten on the right-hand side. Multiplying O_2 on the left-hand side by 5 gives the balanced symbol equation:

C_3H_8 + $5O_2$ → $3CO_2$ + $4H_2O$

Polymers and polymerisation

Revised

Many small molecules (**monomers**) can be joined together to make **polymers** in a process called **polymerisation**.

Some common polymers and their monomers are shown in the table.

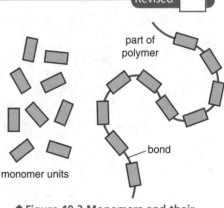

part of polymer

bond

monomer units

↑ **Figure 10.3 Monomers and their polymer**

Polymer	Monomer sub-unit	Uses
polythene	ethene	plastic bags, plastic bottles, clingfilm
polypropene	propene	plastic chairs, detergent bottles, ropes
PVC (polyvinyl chloride)	vinyl chloride	conservatory frames, window frames, drain pipes

The same basic principles apply when writing symbol (structural) equations for polymerisation reactions. There are a few key points:

● the monomer must have a double bond (e.g. C = C)

● we start with 'n' molecules of the monomer – n is a large number

● the polymer has a single bond between the two carbon atoms

● the polymer is written in square brackets and has 'n' after it to show that the polymer repeats what is shown in the brackets n times.

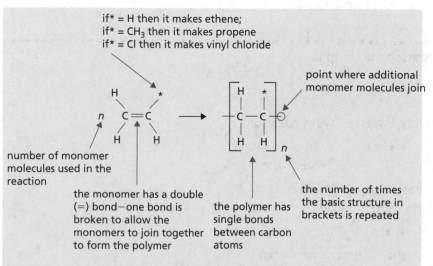

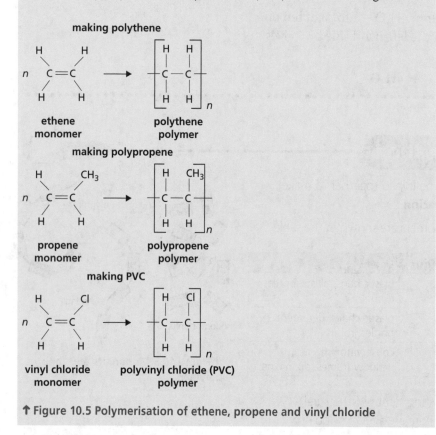

if* = H then it makes ethene;
if* = CH₃ then it makes propene
if* = Cl then it makes vinyl chloride

point where additional monomer molecules join

number of monomer molecules used in the reaction

the monomer has a double (=) bond—one bond is broken to allow the monomers to join together to form the polymer

the polymer has single bonds between carbon atoms

the number of times the basic structure in brackets is repeated

↑ Figure 10.4 The general reaction for polymerisation

The equations for the polymerisation of ethene (making polythene), propene (polypropene) and vinyl chloride (PVC) are shown in Figure 10.5.

making polythene

ethene monomer

polythene polymer

making polypropene

propene monomer

polypropene polymer

making PVC

vinyl chloride monomer

polyvinyl chloride (PVC) polymer

↑ Figure 10.5 Polymerisation of ethene, propene and vinyl chloride

Exam tip

Polymerisation equations are commonly asked for in exams – you are often given the monomer structure and asked to complete polymerisation. Do not forget to add the 'n' and change the double bond to a single bond between the two C atoms. It is also important to show the horizontal lines extending through the brackets.

Types of plastic

There are two main types of plastic as shown in the table.

Type of plastic	Property	Examples
thermoplastic plastics (thermoplastics)	can be repeatedly moulded into different shapes by heating	polythene, polypropene, PVC
thermosetting plastics (thermosets)	cannot be remoulded after the initial setting	bakelite, epoxy resin

When recycling plastics, thermoplastics and thermosets have to be kept separate because they are treated differently in the recycling process due to their properties.

Exam tip

Thermoplastic objects can be remoulded into any new thermoplastic product. Thermoset plastic objects are more difficult to recycle because they cannot be remoulded.

There are many different materials – they can be broadly grouped:

● **Natural materials** – these are not made by processes involving chemical methods – for example granite and wood; they can be obtained from living things such as cotton, wool and silk.

● **Synthetic (man-made) materials** – these involve being processed by chemical methods, e.g. plastics.

Some of the main types of materials and their properties are summarised in the table.

Type	Metals	Plastics	Fibres	Ceramics
Properties	• strong, hard and high density, not flexible • good conductors of heat and electricity • high melting point	• strong and hard (thermosets and thermoplastics) or flexible (thermoplastics) • have a low density • poor conductors of electricity or heat • low melting point	• flexible (not strong or hard) • low density • poor conductors of electricity • low melting point	• strong, hard • high density • not flexible • unreactive • poor conductors of electricity • high melting point
Uses	building; kitchen utensils; electrical wiring; engines	making chairs; bottles; windows frames; doors; clingfilm; covers for electronic devices	clothes; curtains; carpets	bricks for building; crockery; cups
Examples	copper; iron; aluminium	PVC; polythene; bakelite	cotton; silk; nylon	pottery; china

Modern man-made materials have many advantages over traditional materials. They usually:

● are cheaper (and easier to process)

● have 'better' properties.

For example, nylon has been used to replace linen in the manufacture of tablecloths and napkins. Linen takes a long time to make and involves many complex processes to convert the flax plants into finished products. In addition, linen creases very easily and is difficult to iron.

This has led to the decline of the Northern Ireland linen industry – an industry that once employed many thousands of people.

Composite materials

A **composite material** combines the **properties** of two (or more) materials to produce a more useful material for a particular function. Reinforced concrete is a composite material – it contains steel rods running through the concrete. Reinforced concrete has much more strength than normal concrete – this is essential for high-rise buildings. Some examples of composite materials are shown in the table.

> **Exam tip**
>
> A composite material combines the best properties of each separate material. For example, reinforced glass is transparent (because of the glass) but very strong (because of the steel).

Composite material	Components	Examples
glass fibre	glass and plastic	loft insulation
reinforced glass	glass with steel wires running through the glass	security/safety glass
reinforced concrete	concrete with steel rods running through the concrete	construction
glass-reinforced plastic	glass (for strength) and plastic (easily moulded and low density)	car bodies and boats
bone	calcium phosphate and protein	animal skeletons

Nanotechnology

Nanotechnology involves technology using extremely small particles – the nanoscale is around 10^{-9} metres, so $1\,nm = 0.000\,000\,001\,m$. Nanotechnology uses materials in the range 1–100 nm.

It involves using nano-sized materials that have different properties compared with 'normal-sized' materials.

Examples include:

● nanoparticles of silver nitrate are used as **wound dressings**. The silver nanoparticles kill bacteria and prevent infection

● nanoparticles of silver are also used in medical **sterilising sprays** and in the beauty industry.

Smart materials

Smart materials change their properties if exposed to changes in **heat** or **light intensity**.

● **thermochromic** paints and dyes change colour when heated – e.g. colour-changing T-shirts

● **photochromic** paints and dyes change colour when exposed to light or to light intensity changes – e.g. sun glasses that become darker in stronger sunlight.

Shape-memory alloys are a particular type of smart material that spring back into their original shape when bent out of shape – this is useful in making spectacles.

Electrolysis

For **electrolysis** to take place, carbon or graphite **electrodes** are immersed in a liquid and connected to a power supply. Carbon and graphite are suitable because they are unreactive. A current flows between the negative electrode (**cathode**) and the positive electrode (**anode**). The liquid undergoing electrolysis must be able to conduct electricity – it must be an **electrolyte**. The electricity decomposes (breaks down) the electrolyte:

● electrolytes have free ions that move and carry charge

● the positive ions (cations) move to the cathode – the negative ions (anions) move to the anode.

● chemical changes happen at the electrodes.

The method of extraction of aluminium using electrolysis is summarised below.

1 The aluminium ore (bauxite) is purified to form aluminium oxide (alumina).

2 The aluminium oxide is dissolved in molten cryolite, which lowers the temperature needed to carry out the process.

3 An aluminium oxide crust keeps the heat in (the process operates at 900 °C).

4 At the negative electrode, positive aluminium ions combine with electrons to form aluminium metal.

5   At the positive electrode, negative oxide ions form oxygen gas.

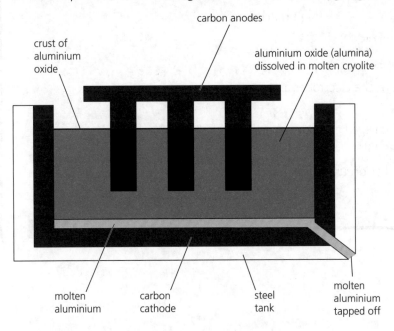

crust of aluminium oxide

carbon anodes

aluminium oxide (alumina) dissolved in molten cryolite

molten aluminium

carbon cathode

steel tank

molten aluminium tapped off

↑ Figure 10.6 Extracting aluminium using electrolysis

The ionic equation for the reaction at the cathode is:

$$Al^{3+} + 3e^- \rightarrow Al$$

Revision questions

Tested

1   Explain the term 'hydrocarbon'.   [2 marks]

2   a) Describe the process of fractional distillation. [3]

    b) Name **three** products of the fractional distillation of crude oil. [3]

    c) Give **one** use for **one** of the products. [1]   [7 marks]

3   The molecular formula of ethane is C_2H_6.

    a) Draw the structural formula of ethane. [1]

    b) Copy and complete the **balanced** symbol equation for the complete combustion of ethane. [2]   [3 marks]

    $$C_2H_6 + O_2 \rightarrow$$

4   a) Give **two** reasons why ceramics are good for making kitchen crockery – plates, cups and saucers. [2]

    b) Give **two** reasons why iron is suitable for use as a frying pan. [2]   [4 marks]

5   a) Describe the process of polymerisation. [2]

    b) Copy and complete the structural equation to show how ethene is made into polythene. [3]   [5 marks]

$$n \quad \begin{matrix} H & & H \\ & \diagdown & \diagup \\ & C = C \\ & \diagup & \diagdown \\ H & & H \end{matrix} \quad \longrightarrow$$

ethene monomer

6 a) Describe fully what is meant by 'nanotechnology'. [2]

  b) Give **one** use of nanotechnology. [1]   **[3 marks]**

7 a) Explain what is meant by the term 'electrolysis'. [2]

  b) Copy and complete the following sentences.

  In the extraction of aluminium from its ore, the electrodes are made of ....

  The aluminium is formed at the .... charged cathode, whereas at the anode, oxide ions form .... gas. [3]

  c) Write an ionic equation for the reaction that occurs at the cathode. [2]   **[7 marks]**

Go online for the answers   Online

11 Hard water, recycling and exploitation of the Earth's resources

Soft and hard water

Revised

Water can be 'hard' or 'soft':

- **soft water** forms a lather easily with soap
- **hard water** does not easily form a lather with soap – it forms a 'scum' instead.

Hard water can have **temporary** hardness or **permanent** hardness.

Temporary hardness can be removed by boiling – the boiling softens the water. Permanent hardness cannot be removed by boiling.

The causes of hardness in water

Hardness in water is caused by at least one of a range of compounds that are dissolved in natural water. Broadly speaking, hardness is caused by calcium ions (Ca^{2+}) or magnesium ions (Mg^{2+}).

Compound	Type of hardness
calcium chloride	permanent
calcium hydrogencarbonate	temporary
magnesium sulfate	permanent
magnesium hydrogencarbonate	temporary
magnesium chloride	permanent

> **Exam tip**
>
> It is important to remember that it is compounds of calcium and magnesium that cause hardness in water.

> **Exam tip**
>
> Note that it is the hydrogencarbonates that cause temporary hardness – the other compounds cause permanent hardness.

Softening hard water

Revised

Temporary hardness can be removed by **boiling**. This causes the calcium hydrogencarbonate/magnesium hydrogencarbonate to break down by **thermal decomposition**.

The word equations for softening temporary hard water are:

calcium hydrogencarbonate → calcium carbonate + carbon dioxide + water

magnesium hydrogencarbonate → magnesium carbonate + carbon dioxide + water

The balanced symbol equations for softening temporary hard water are:

$$Ca(HCO_3)_2 \rightarrow CaCO_3 + CO_2 + H_2O$$
$$Mg(HCO_3)_2 \rightarrow MgCO_3 + CO_2 + H_2O$$

The equations show that softening temporary hard water by boiling produces calcium carbonate or magnesium carbonate. These are insoluble solids that can cause **limescale** deposits (fur) inside kettles, hot water tanks and hot water pipes. The furring of pipes reduces the water flow and kettle elements may not work if too much limescale is present.

> **Exam tip**
>
> You should know that limescale formation occurs in kettles, hot water tanks and hot water pipes because household water can be very hot. The heat breaks down the calcium hydrogencarbonate or magnesium hydrogencarbonate (thermal decomposition) into calcium carbonate or magnesium carbonate, both of which are insoluble (and cause the furring), along with carbon dioxide and water.

Carbonates and hydrogencarbonates

Calcium carbonate ($CaCO_3$) and magnesium carbonate ($MgCO_3$) react with hydrochloric acid as shown in the word equations below. These reactions can be used to remove limescale from hot water pipes and so on.

calcium carbonate + hydrochloric acid → calcium chloride + carbon dioxide + water

magnesium carbonate + hydrochloric acid → magnesium chloride + carbon dioxide + water

The balanced symbol equations for these reactions are:

$CaCO_3 + 2HCl \rightarrow CaCl_2 + CO_2 + H_2O$

$MgCO_3 + 2HCl \rightarrow MgCl_2 + CO_2 + H_2O$

Worked example

a) Explain what causes scaly deposits (fur) in kettles.

b) Explain how it can be removed.

Answer

a) Heat (in hot water) breaks down calcium hydrogencarbonate/ magnesium hydrogencarbonate in temporary hard water. This forms calcium/magnesium carbonate (plus carbon dioxide and water) which are insoluble. These cause limescale to be deposited.

b) Add hydrochloric acid to the calcium/magnesium carbonate. This breaks down the carbonate to form calcium/magnesium chloride (which are soluble), carbon dioxide and water.

Softening permanent hard water

Boiling has no effect on permanent hard water, so other methods must be used to soften it.

Ion exchange is one such method – the calcium ions (Ca^{2+}) and magnesium ions (Mg^{2+}) that cause hard water are removed and the water is softened.

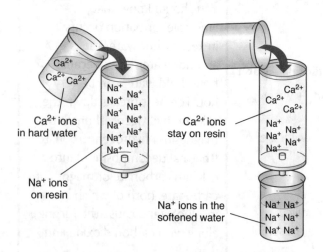

↑ **Figure 11.1 Softening hard water by ion exchange**

The hard water is poured into an ion-exchange column. Inside the column sodium ions (Na^+) are attached to resin-coated beads.

As the water flows over the beads the calcium/magnesium ions are exchanged with sodium ions. The water that leaves the column has sodium ions (that do not cause hardness) but the calcium/magnesium ions are retained in the ion-exchange column.

Another method of softening hard water is **distillation** – this involves heating (evaporating) and condensing the water as shown in Figure 11.2. The water evaporates leaving the calcium and magnesium compounds behind in the flask. The water that condenses in the condenser is soft.

Exam tip

There are similarities between the distillation of hard water and the fractional distillation of crude oil. Both involve heating and evaporating liquids followed by collecting the liquid(s) after condensation.

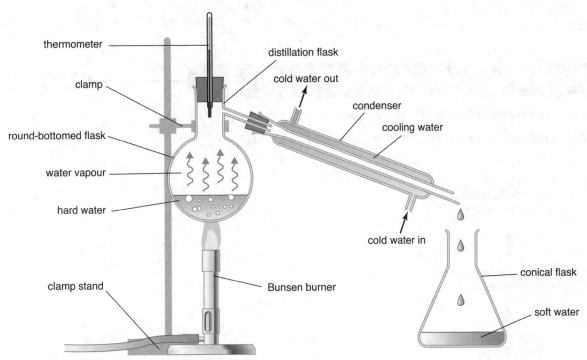

↑ **Figure 11.2 Softening hard water by distillation**

Another chemical method of softening hard water involves **washing soda** – this is sodium carbonate (Na_2CO_3). The washing soda dissolves and the carbonate ions ions join with the calcium/magnesium ions in the hard water to form calcium carbonate/magnesium carbonate. Calcium carbonate and magnesium carbonate are solids and because they are insoluble in water they are no longer dissolved in it – so the hard water is now soft.

A word equation for using washing soda to soften hard water caused by calcium ions is:

calcium chloride + sodium carbonate → calcium carbonate + sodium chloride

The calcium carbonate is a solid – a solid that results when two solutions react is called a **precipitate** – the reaction is a **precipitation reaction**.

Hard water regions

Areas that have limestone rocks and/or chalk rocks have hard water. Calcium ions and magnesium ions are formed from reactions between the rock and rainwater. As a result of the reactions, the chalk or limestone is chemically worn away to produce the geological features characteristic of hard water regions.

Exam tip

Ion exchange, distillation and washing soda remove both temporary and permanent hardness from water. However, they are mainly used to remove permanent hardness because boiling is easier and cheaper if removing temporary hardness.

Hard water regions typically have **caves**, **stalagmites** and **stalactites**, which help in promoting **tourism** – like the Marble Arch caves in County Fermanagh.

The advantages and disadvantages of hard water are summarised in this table.

Advantages	Disadvantages
• better taste • stronger bones and teeth (due to the calcium ions) • good for making beer • good for tourism	• furring water pipes/kettles/hot water tanks • staining clothes • difficult to form a lather with soap • dishwasher salt needed in dishwashers

Recycling and exploitation of Earth's resources
Revised

Materials that can be **recycled** include plastic, iron, paper and tin cans.

It is important to **reduce**, **reuse** and **recycle** as explained in Figure 11.3 below.

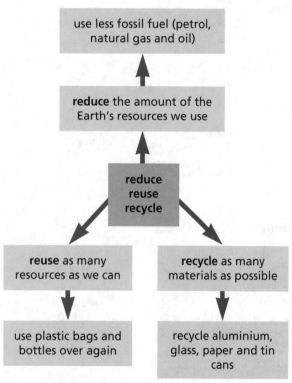

↑ Figure 11.3 Reduce, reuse and recycle

The benefits of recycling

It is important to **recycle** many materials for three main reasons:

● It stops **non-renewable resources** running out. Many resources, such as fossil fuels, are non-renewable – this means they cannot be made again in a short time.

● It **saves energy** compared to making new products from scratch. Producing energy usually involves the burning of fossil fuels in power stations. The carbon dioxide produced contributes to global warming.

● **Landfill sites** for dumping waste are running out. In addition, they produce lots of methane (a greenhouse gas) as well as being unsightly and polluting the ground.

Exam tip

The second and third bullet points are **environmental** advantages for recycling.

Promoting recycling

The Government promotes recycling through local councils. Each council has a **target** for recycling so much material. Councils can get fined if they do not reach these recycling targets.

Recycling is encouraged by councils in many ways:

- They provide **separate bins** that are colour coded for household refuse – many households have separate bins for general waste, recyclables such as tin cans, paper and garden and food waste.

- **Separating metal, iron and steel** items from general waste – these can be taken to a municipal collection centre for recycling.

- Producing **mulch** from garden waste – grass cuttings can be kept in a compost heap at the end of the garden. In time, the grass cuttings (and other garden waste) break down to form compost, which can be used as fertiliser. This is also what councils do with the compostable waste they collect.

- Making a **charge** on businesses for putting waste in landfill sites.

Worked example

Describe and explain **one** advantage of charging businesses for putting waste in landfill sites.

Answer

It reduces waste in landfill sites because land for such sites is running out – they also cause pollution and are unsightly, often attracting vermin and causing nasty odours.

or Encourages businesses to recycle more waste – this saves energy and other resources.

or Raises money that can be used to promote recycling or other environmental initiatives.

Glass recycling

A lot of waste is glass (glass bottles and jars). The recycling of glass is summarised in Figure 11.4. The used glass is **collected** (often in bottle banks) and broken up into small pieces called **cullet**. It is then **melted** and **remoulded** to form new glass products.

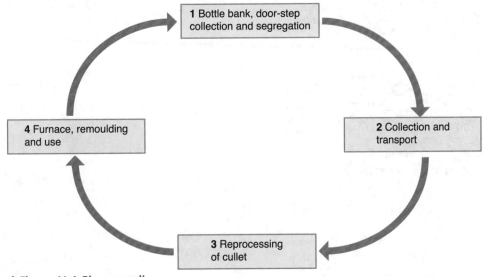

↑ **Figure 11.4 Glass recycling**

Biodegradable and non-biodegradable materials

Biodegradable materials can be broken down by **microorganisms** (bacteria and fungi). Garden waste is biodegradable, as is food waste. Some rubbish bins are dedicated to biodegradable material. Plastics, glass and metal are not biodegradable.

Recycling plastics

Thermosetting plastics cannot be remoulded – they can be reused, but not recycled into a different plastic object.

Thermoplastics can be melted and remoulded – they can be reused or recycled into different plastic objects.

Making a hard, biodegradable polymer (plastic)

Scientists are making new types of plastic that are biodegradable. One such plastic is made from starch powder – potatoes are very rich in starch. Starch is a branched polymer of **glucose** molecules. The process involves two steps:

1 The **starch** is treated with hydrochloric acid (HCl) – this removes the branches, allowing the chains to pack closer to each other forming a plastic.

2 Adding **glycerol** stops the chains getting too close and keeps the plastic flexible – the glycerol is described as a **plasticiser**.

The process is shown in Figure 11.5.

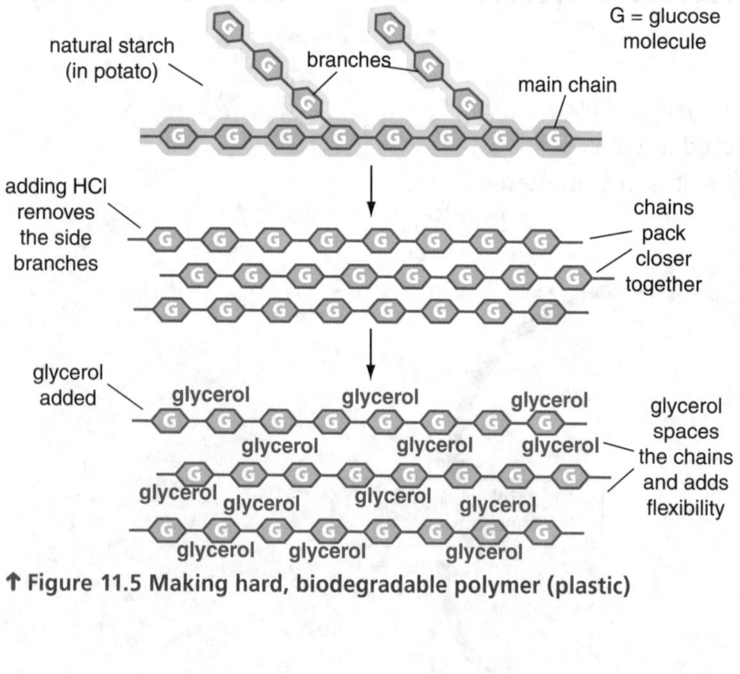

> ## Exam tip
> Both types of plastic can be reused, but only thermoplastics can be remoulded. It is important to avoid putting plastic in landfill because it is usually non-biodegradable.

↑ Figure 11.5 Making hard, biodegradable polymer (plastic)

1 The following table shows the results of an investigation testing the hardness of water in four different water samples.

Water sample	Volume of soap solution needed to form a lather before boiling/cm³	Volume of soap solution needed to form a lather after boiling/cm³
A	25	25
B	28	10
C	3	3
D	25	3

a) Which water sample is the least hard? [1]

b) Which water sample contains only temporary hardness? [1]

c) Which water sample contains permanent hardness? [1]

d) Which water sample contains both temporary and permanent hardness? [1]

e) i) Copy and complete the word equation for a reaction that breaks down temporary hardness:

magnesium hydrogencarbonate → [3]

ii) This reaction involves thermal decomposition. Explain what is meant by 'thermal decomposition'. [2] **[9 marks]**

2 Explain fully how hard water can be softened by distillation. **[3 marks]**

3 a) Hard water forms deposits of calcium carbonate (fur) in hot water pipes. Copy and complete the balanced symbol equation for this reaction:

$Ca(HCO_3)_2 \rightarrow$ _____ + _____ + _____ [3]

b) Explain how the fur can be removed. [3] **[6 marks]**

4 The graph shows the percentage of household waste that has been recycled from a large city over ten years.

a) Calculate the increase in the percentage of waste recycled between 2000 and 2010. [2]

b) Give **one** reason why it is important to increase the amount of material recycled. [1]

c) Suggest what happens to garden waste after it is collected by a council. [1] **[3 marks]**

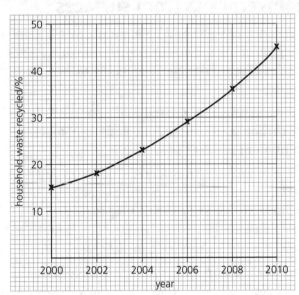

5 Describe the process of glass recycling. **[3 marks]**

12 Using materials to fight crime

Science can be used to prevent crime and also to help solve crimes – this is forensic science.

Fingerprints
Revised

Everyone has a pattern of fine lines (a **fingerprint**) on their fingertips. There are four main types of fingerprint pattern – these are **arch**, **loop**, **whorl** and **composite**.

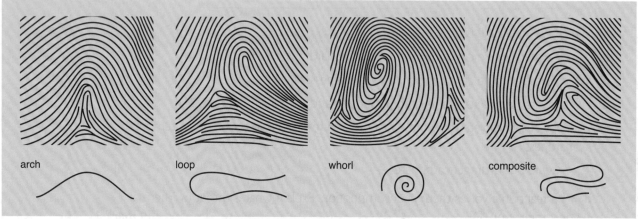

arch   loop   whorl   composite

↑ **Figure 12.1 The four types of fingerprints**

However, every person has a **unique** fingerprint pattern (no two people have the same fingerprint). This is what makes fingerprinting so valuable in criminal trials.

Obtaining fingerprints from surfaces

If you press your fingertips against a hard surface you leave a fingerprint on that surface. Fingerprints on surfaces are normally invisible. Scientific techniques are needed to get a fingerprint and make it visible. There are several stages involved:

1 The fingerprint marks have to be **dusted** with a powder. If the surface is **white**, black **carbon** powder is used. If the surface is **black** or **mirrored**, **aluminium** powder is used.

2 Once dusted, the fingerprint is **transferred**. The excess dust is brushed off and sticky tape is pressed over the fingerprint. The dust sticks to the sticky tape and it can then be transferred to a card. Carbon prints are transferred to white card (for contrast) and aluminium powder prints are transferred to black card.

3 The fingerprints can be **compared** with the previously-taken fingerprints of suspects. For over 100 years fingerprints have been used in the court system. Because fingerprints are unique, they can be used to help prove both guilt and innocence.

> **Exam tip**
>
> In questions about taking fingerprints, make sure you describe dusting, transferring and comparing.

Genetic fingerprinting (DNA profiling)

Everyone has unique DNA. This can be used in the same way as traditional fingerprints to prove innocence or guilt.

- DNA can be obtained from body cells – these can be found in blood, hair, skin and other body fluids.
- The DNA sample is amplified (many exact copies are made).
- The DNA sample is chemically treated and cut up into small fragments (bands).
- The fragments are separated by passing an electrical current through a gel. This separation gives the characteristic banded appearance of genetic fingerprints.

Figure 12.2 shows a genetic fingerprint taken from a crime scene and the genetic fingerprints of two suspects. The fingerprint taken from the scene is exactly the same as suspect B (but not suspect A). This evidence links suspect B to the crime scene.

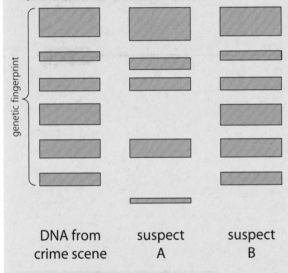

DNA from crime scene   suspect A   suspect B

↑ **Figure 12.2 DNA profiling – comparing genetic fingerprints**

Genetic fingerprint data can be easily stored in a **national database**. In many countries people who have been convicted of a crime have their DNA stored by the police. There are arguments for and against everyone having their DNA fingerprint held on a database.

Worked example

a) Give **one** advantage of using DNA profiling (genetic fingerprints) compared to traditional fingerprints.

b) Give **one** argument for and **one** argument against having everyone's DNA fingerprint stored in a national database.

Answers

a) Any **one** of: DNA can be obtained from any body tissue, not just the fingertips; it is easier to compare the DNA fingerprints of different people (rather than comparing 'traditional' fingerprints); DNA comparisons are more 'scientific' and can give a higher level of certainty.

b) *For* – would make crime detection much easier
Against – civil liberties; innocent people would have their genetic fingerprint on a DNA database.

Clothing fibres and crime

There are many different types of fibre used in making clothing. Comparing fibres left at the scene of a crime with fibres from a suspect's clothing can be used in the same way as fingerprints.

The fibres can be compared using powerful microscopes. Nylon, wool and cotton can be identified easily. The types of properties that can be used when comparing the fibres in clothing include:

- the relative proportions of the different fibres
- the way the garment is knitted or woven
- the colours of the fibres
- stains within the fibres – e.g. sweat.

Hair is also a natural fibre – comparison of hair samples can be used in confirming if someone was at the scene of a crime or not. Hair from different people can differ in length, colour, thickness, tendency to curl among many other ways.

Exam tip

Evidence provided by fibres is not as conclusive as either type of fingerprint – for example more than one person may have the same type of jumper. However, hair can provide excellent evidence – as well as normal hair features such as colour, it can also provide a genetic fingerprint.

Crime prevention

As well as solving crimes, it is important to prevent crime happening in the first place if possible.

Preventing the forgery of banknotes

It is very important to stop bank notes being forged. If it was easy to forge bank notes, many people would try it!

Bank notes are protected against forgery by:

- the special quality of the paper used
- the hologram
- watermarks
- bar codes
- the metal strip
- special ink.

Shops can protect against the use of forged notes by using ultraviolet (UV) light to scan notes. If a note is forged it will fluoresce – genuine notes do not fluoresce.

Exam tip

In exam questions it is important that you are clear about whether you are being asked about features of bank notes that prevent forgery, or the way in which shops can detect forged notes.

Preventing crime in the home

There are many ways of protecting valuables in the home. These include:

- fitting alarm systems
- keeping doors and windows locked
- marking valuables with a security pen
- cancelling papers/deliveries when on holiday
- asking neighbours to keep an eye on the house when you are away.

Metal ions produce a coloured flame when heated in a Bunsen flame, this is called a flame test. A flame test can be used to identify metal ions found at the scene of a crime. They can be compared to those found on a suspect's clothing. It is important to wear safety goggles and to take care when using a Bunsen burner.

These are the steps for carrying out a flame test:

1 Clean the flame-test rod in hydrochloric acid and heat it in a Bunsen flame.

2 Dip the end of the cleaned rod in the sample solution (containing the metal ions) and then hold the rod in the flame.

3 Observe and record the colour change.

4 The rod must be cleaned between samples.

The flame-test colours of a range of metal ions are shown in the table.

Metal	Metal ion	Flame colour
lithium	Li^+	red
sodium	Na^+	orange-yellow
potassium	K^+	lilac
calcium	Ca^{2+}	brick-red
lead	Pb^{2+}	blue-white
copper	Cu^{2+}	blue-green

Emission spectroscopy is a more effective method of identifying the presence of metal ions. The spectrum produced from ions at a crime scene can be compared against a database.

Exam tip

Emission spectroscopy is more accurate because it does not depend on observer judgement – as identifying colours in a flame test does.

Revision questions

1 Describe how you would take a fingerprint from the door of a black car. **[4 marks]**

2 Police were investigating a stolen car. They found some clothes fibres on the driver's seat.

   a) State **two** features of the fibres that they could use to try to identify the person who stole the car. [2]

   b) Explain why the evidence from the fibres will probably not be as good as fingerprint evidence. [1] **[3 marks]**

3 a) State **three** things you can do to protect valuables in the home. [3]

   b) Give **three** ways in which bank notes are protected against forgery. [3] **[6 marks]**

4 Copy and complete the table below about flame tests. **[3 marks]**

Metal	Flame colour
lithium	
	orange-yellow
potassium	

Go online for the answers

Online

13 Electrical circuits

Electrical circuits

Electricity can flow in an electric circuit. **Circuit diagrams** can be used to represent electric circuits. Figure 13.1 shows the symbols for the main components in an electrical circuit.

Component	Symbol	Function
battery		to supply electricity
bulb		to convert current to light
switch		to control the flow of current
fuse		to stop too much current flowing
voltmeter	V	to measure voltage
ammeter	A	to measure current
resistor		to cut down the amount of current flowing

↑ **Figure 13.1 Circuit symbols**

Circuit diagrams

Figure 13.2 shows a very simple electric circuit with one battery and one bulb.

Voltage and current

Voltage is the amount of electrical energy supplied to a circuit (or a component). Batteries supply voltage – a voltage is measured using a **voltmeter** and the unit of voltage is the **volt** (**V**). A 12 V battery provides more electricity than a 5 V battery.

Current is the amount of electricity flowing around a circuit (or through a component). Current is measured using an **ammeter** and the unit of current is the **amp** (**A**).

Electric circuits can be arranged in series or in parallel.

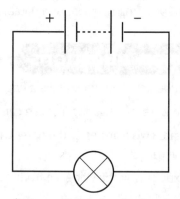

↑ **Figure 13.2 A simple electric circuit**

> **Exam tip**
>
> Electricity will only flow if a circuit is complete with no gaps.

> **Exam tip**
>
> A battery is two or more (electrical) cells – they can provide more electricity than a single cell. The battery in Figure 13.2 has two cells.

Series circuits

The components (e.g. bulbs) are connected side-by-side as shown in Figure 13.3.

In the diagram the switch is open – the circuit is incomplete – so the bulbs will not light. When the switch is closed, both bulbs will light.

In a series circuit, the total voltage is shared between the bulbs. In the circuit in Figure 13.3, each bulb receives half the voltage (assuming the two bulbs are identical).

In a series circuit, the current does not change around the circuit. This means that in the circuit in Figure 13.3 each bulb will have the same brightness (assuming they are identical).

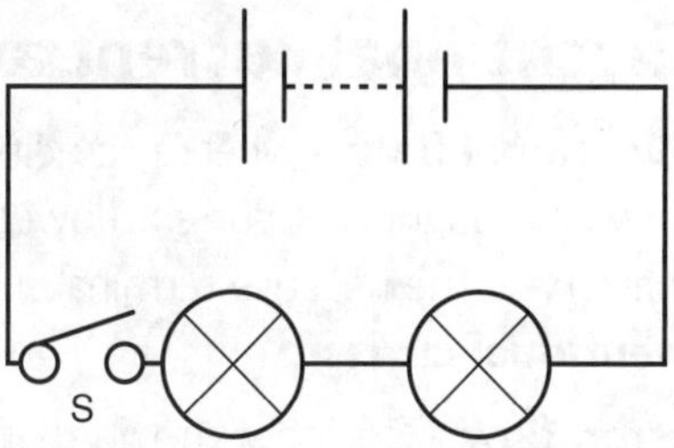

Parallel circuits

In parallel circuits there is more than one branch through which electricity can flow. Figure 13.4 shows two bulbs connected in parallel.

In Figure 13.4 if switch S_1 is closed, only the upper bulb will light because current will flow through only the upper branch of the circuit. If both switches (S_1 and S_2) are closed, both bulbs will light. If only S_2 is closed then only the lower bulb will light.

In a parallel circuit, each bulb (or branch of the circuit) receives the total voltage from the battery.

In a parallel circuit, the current is shared between the branches.

Measuring voltage and current

When measuring the voltage across a component – e.g. a bulb – the voltmeter is connected in parallel with it.

When measuring the current through a component – e.g. bulb – the ammeter is placed in series. See Figure 13.5.

Worked example

Figure 13.5 represents an electric circuit containing two cells and three identical bulbs.

a) Describe how the bulbs are arranged.

b) Ammeter A_1 has a reading of 6 A. What will be the reading on ammeter A_2?

c) Voltmeter V_1 has a reading of 12 V. What will be the reading on voltmeter V_2?

d) Give **one** change that will take place if more batteries are added to the circuit.

Answer

a) parallel

b) 2 A – the current is shared among the three branches in a parallel circuit (6 A ÷ 3 = 2 A).

c) 12 V – each branch receives the total voltage in a parallel circuit.

d) Any **one** of: increased voltage; increased current; increased brightness of bulbs.

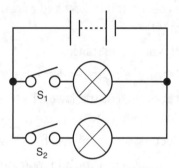

↑ Figure 13.3 Two bulbs connected in series

Exam tip

If Figure 13.3 had three bulbs, each would get one third of the voltage supplied by the battery.

↑ Figure 13.4 Two bulbs connected in parallel

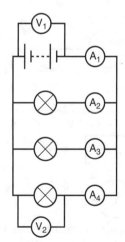

↑ Figure 13.5 A circuit with three bulbs

Conventional current and electron flow

Conventional flow – when electricity was first studied, about 200 years ago, it was thought that current flowed from the positive terminal of a cell/battery to the negative terminal. This is known as the direction of **conventional current**.

Electron flow – it is now known that electricity is actually electrons flowing from the negative terminal of a cell to the positive terminal. Being negative particles, electrons are repelled from the negative terminal and attracted to the positive terminal.

Resistance

Revised

Circuits and their components resist (oppose) the electric current flowing through them – this is described as **resistance**. The unit of resistance is the **ohm (Ω)**.

Some facts about resistance:

- the bigger the resistance, less current can flow
- insulators, such plastic, have a high resistance that prevents electricity flowing through them
- conductors, such as metals, have low resistance
- in a series circuit, if you add more bulbs the bulbs get dimmer – this is because each time a bulb is added there is more resistance.

Calculating resistance

Voltage (V), current (I) and resistance (R) are linked by the equation:

$$V = I \times R \quad \left(or\ R = \frac{V}{I}\right)$$

You can calculate resistance by measuring the voltage and the current in a circuit, and then use the formula $R = \frac{V}{I}$.

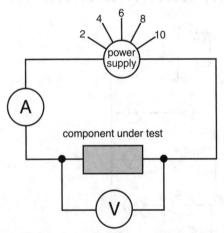

↑ **Figure 13.6 Measuring resistance: the ammeter–voltmeter method**

Factors affecting the resistance of a wire

- **Length** – the longer a wire is, the more wire there is to resist the current. If the length of wire is doubled, the resistance is doubled and so on. The resistance of a wire is **directly proportional** to its length.

- **Material** – the lower the resistance it has, the better a conductor is. This is why copper is commonly used in circuits. Wires often used to demonstrate resistance are **constantan** (a mixture of nickel and copper) and **nichrome** (a mixture of nickel and chromium).

- Cross-sectional area – the thicker the wire is, the smaller is its resistance. If the cross-sectional area is doubled, the resistance will halve and so on. The resistance of a wire is inversely proportional to its cross-sectional area.

Fixed and variable resistors

Fixed resistors are used to limit the size of current flowing through a component or round a circuit.

Variable resistors (rheostats) are used for changing the current flowing through a component or round a circuit. Variable resistors are used in dimmer-light switches and in sound-volume controls in radios and televisions.

Figure 13.7 shows the symbols for the different resistors.

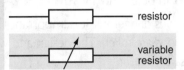
↑ **Figure 13.7 The symbols for fixed and variable resistors**

The heating effect of resistance

Because resistance opposes the flow of electricity, heat is generated. The heat produced by resistance is used in kettles, toasters, hairdryers and many other appliances. In these, certain sections of the electric circuit (elements) have a very high resistance that can generate considerable heat.

Revision questions
Tested

1 The diagram below shows two electrical circuits.

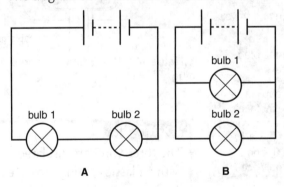

a) In which circuit are the bulbs connected in parallel? [1]

b) If the batteries supply 6 V, what will be the voltage across bulb 2 in each circuit? Explain your answer. [4]

c) What will happen in each circuit if bulb 2 becomes loose? [2]   **[7 marks]**

2 Describe how you would measure the current in a simple series electric circuit.   **[2 marks]**

3 A bulb in an electric circuit has a voltage of 5 V and a current of 1.25 A. Calculate the resistance.   **[2 marks]**

4 a) Describe how you could investigate the effect of the cross-sectional area of a wire on its resistance. [4]

   b) State two things you would need to keep the same in this investigation. [2]   **[6 marks]**

Go online for the answers
Online

14 Household electricity

Why is electricity so useful?

Electricity is relatively easily distributed to homes and businesses. It can be transferred into other forms of useful energy easily. These include:

- **heat** in irons, ovens and toasters
- **movement** (kinetic) in fans, washing machine and tumble dryer motors
- **sound** in radios, televisions and electric doorbells
- **light** in bulbs and TV screens

Electricity is dangerous. It is important that all the necessary safety precautions are taken. The design and wiring of a three-pin plug shows many safety features.

Safety and electricity

A three-pin plug connects an appliance to a socket – it has many safety features.

The three-pin plug

Figure 14.1 shows the wiring inside a three-pin plug.

Colour	Name	Connection	Function
brown	live	right terminal	electricity enters the plug and travels to the appliance
blue	neutral	left terminal	returns the electricity to the plug socket from an appliance
yellow and green	earth	top terminal	if a fault develops in an appliance that has metal parts, the metal can conduct electricity – the earth wire is an escape route allowing the electricity to flow to Earth and not through someone touching the appliance!

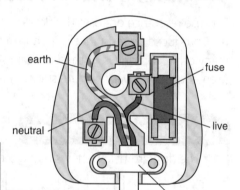

↑ **Figure 14.1 The wiring in a three-pin plug**

Safety features of the three-pin plug

These include:

- the casing of the plug is made of **plastic**, an insulator
- the **cable grip** prevents the cable from being pulled out
- the **fuse** protects the appliance and the user.

Fuses

Fuses are short lengths of safety wire that stop too much current flowing in a circuit. They are very important **safety** devices.

> **Exam tip**
>
> The three wires are insulated with a plastic coating. However, if you are asked to name a safety feature in a plug you may not get credit for this – this is because this safety feature is not actually part of the plug.

> **Exam tip**
>
> The fuse is on the live side of the plug – if the fuse blows, this will stop electricity reaching the appliance and the user.

This is how a fuse works:

1 The more current in the fuse wire, the hotter it becomes.

2 If the current is too high, the fuse wire melts ('blows').

3 The circuit is no longer complete (there is a gap).

4 This stops the flow of current and protects the appliance and the user.

Common fuse sizes are 1 A, 2 A, 3 A, 5 A and 13 A – the correct fuse must be used for each appliance:

● the fuse should not melt when the normal current is flowing through the circuit

● the fuse should melt when the current rises just above the normal level.

The formula:

$$\text{power } (P) = \text{voltage } (V) \times \text{current } (I)$$

can be used to calculate the current normally flowing through an appliance. The units of power are **watts (W)** or **kilowatts (kW)** 1000 W = 1 kW.

$P = V \times I$ can be rearranged as $I = \dfrac{P}{V}$ or $V = \dfrac{P}{I}$

Exam tip

When using the formula, power must be in watts. If you are given power as kilowatts, you must convert this to watts (× 1000) before using the formula.

Worked example

Find the fuse required for a 60 W lamp working at a mains voltage of 220 V.

Answer

Power = 60 W and voltage = 220 V

$$I = \frac{P}{V}$$

$$= \frac{60}{220} = 0.73 \text{ A}$$

So it is best to use a 1 A fuse – it is just bigger than the current normally needed by the appliance.

Exam tip

Too small a fuse will not carry enough current for the appliance to work properly – it will blow even if the appliance is working properly.

Exam tip

Too large a fuse will allow too much current to flow in the event of a fault putting the appliance and the user at risk.

Other electrical safety features

Double insulation – many electrical appliances (e.g. computers) have plastic casings that cannot give an electric shock, even if there is a fault inside. These appliances have their metal parts in a separate plastic container, within the outer plastic cover – they are **double insulated**. Such appliances do not need a plug with an earth wire.

Residual circuit breakers – these detect faults in appliances and switch off, breaking the circuit and preventing the flow of current. In modern houses they are built into circuits. Unlike fuses that need replacing if they blow, residual circuit breakers can be reset easily. They also work more quickly than fuses as a safety device.

The cost of electricity

From information provided, you need to be able to calculate how much electricity is used over a period of time and how much it costs.

Electricity meters are used to show how much electricity a house or business uses. Electric-providing companies refer to '**units**' of electricity. Each unit costs a certain amount, so:

electric bill = number of units used × cost of each unit

The unit of electricity is the **kilowatt-hour (kWh)**. This is the amount of electricity used by an appliance that uses 1000 W of power for 1 hour.

The cost of electricity used by an appliance can be calculated using the formula:

energy (kWh) = power (kW) × time (h)

> **Exam tip**
>
> Many examination questions show the meter readings at the start and the end of a billing period. You can work out the cost by calculating the difference in the readings (the number of units used) and multiplying this by the cost of each unit.

Worked example

Calculate the cost of using a cooker ring with a power of 2000 W for 2 hours if the cost of electricity is 10 pence per kWh.

Answer
Power = 2000 W = 2 kW; time = 2 h

Energy used = 2 × 2

$\qquad$ = 4 kWh

Cost = 4 × 10 p = 40 p

> **Exam tip**
>
> In this formula the power is in kW. Many candidates forget to convert information given in watts to kilowatts, in questions about electricity costs.

Saving electricity

You can reduce your electricity bills by using less electricity. You can do this by:

● turning off electrical equipment when it is not in use – for example not leaving the television on 'stand-by'

● using low-energy light bulbs

● turning off lights when a room is not being used

● buying energy-efficient appliances.

> **Exam tip**
>
> It is important to use your common sense when describing ways of saving electricity. Answering 'do not use the lights' is not realistic and will not gain credit. However, 'switching off the lights when no one is in the room' will gain credit.

Making electricity

Moving a **magnet** inside a coil of wire makes electricity and generates a current in the wire.

Figure 14.2 shows a simple dynamo – the rotation of the magnet produces electricity in the coils of wire.

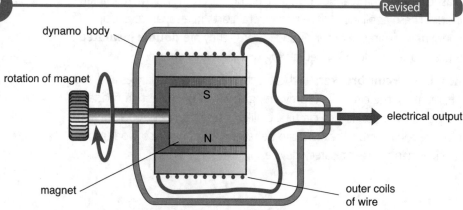

↑ Figure 14.2 Generating electricity using a dynamo

Power stations

The same principle is used in generating electrical energy in power stations. The key difference is that power stations make much more electricity.

Figure 14 .3 shows the main parts of a power station.

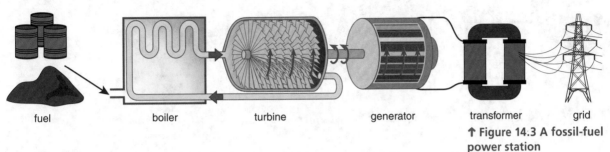

fuel   boiler   turbine   generator   transformer   grid

↑ **Figure 14.3 A fossil-fuel power station**

The function of the different parts of a power station are summarised in the table.

Component	Function	Energy change
burner	the fuel is burned to produce heat	chemical energy in fossil fuels is transferred to heat (thermal) energy
boiler	heat is used to turn water into steam	thermal energy is used to boil water forming steam (kinetic energy)
turbine	the steam drives the turbine, which is connected to the generator	the kinetic energy of steam is transferred to kinetic energy of the turbine
generator	the rotating generator (large dynamo) makes the electricity	kinetic energy is transferred to electrical energy

Electricity transmission

Electricity has to be transmitted from where it is made (power stations) to houses and businesses around the country. The electricity is distributed through a **grid** of power lines.

The electricity being transmitted in the (national) grid:

● is transmitted at high voltage (e.g. 275 kV or 400 kV)

● has a relatively low current

● is often carried in power lines suspended from high pylons for safety because the high voltages used are very dangerous.

The high voltages used allow the electricity to flow with a relatively low current and transfers less energy as waste heat. It also allows thinner (and cheaper) power lines to be used.

Transformers

A typical power station generates electricity at about 30 kV. This is then converted to the grid voltage (usually 275 kV or 400 kV) using a **step-up transformer**. Before the electricity can be used in homes or businesses, the voltage is reduced using a **step-down transformer**.

● Step-up transformer – increases the voltage and decreases the current (to reduce energy (heat) losses).

● Step-down transformer – decreases the voltage and increases the current.

Figure 14.4 shows the relative positions of step-up and step-down transformers in the electricity grid.

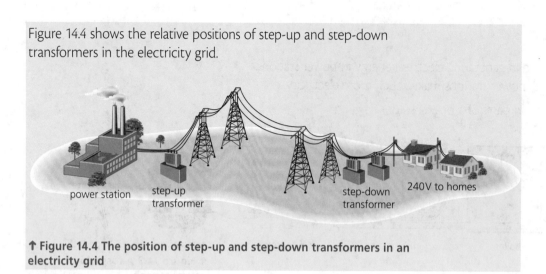

power station   step-up transformer   step-down transformer   240V to homes

↑ **Figure 14.4 The position of step-up and step-down transformers in an electricity grid**

Renewable energy

Revised

Fossil fuels (such as coal, oil and gas) are **non-renewable** because they will run out – and they cannot be replaced quickly.

Renewable energy sources will not run out – these include wind, solar, hydroelectric and tidal power.

In recent years there has been an increasing emphasis on developing the use of renewable forms of energy for two main reasons:

● non-renewables are running out

● non-renewable energy, such as from the use of fossil fuels, produce large amounts of carbon dioxide – this contributes to **global warming**.

The advantages and disadvantages of using different types of renewable energy are summarised in the table.

Renewable source	Method	Advantages	Disadvantages
wind	• blades of wind turbines rotate • and drive a generator	• renewable • does not pollute the atmosphere • wind is free	• noisy and ugly • often sited in remote areas • work only when wind blows
hydroelectric	• water flows downhill from a reservoir • a rotating turbine turns a generator	• once built, very cost effective • does not pollute the atmosphere • water is free	• land is flooded to create the reservoir • habitats are destroyed • farming land is lost
tidal	• tides (coming in and out) drive a turbine • which turns a generator	• once built, very cost effective • water is free • does not pollute the atmosphere	• only work when the tide is coming in or out • can harm wildlife

> **Exam tip**
>
> If you are asked to give an **environmental** advantage or disadvantage of an energy source you must only give environmental answers – for example 'does not pollute the atmosphere', 'harms wildlife' – and not answers such as 'water is cheap'.
>
> Solar energy works in a different way to those in the table, where turbines are driven. Solar cells convert light energy into electricity. Solar energy is renewable, non-polluting and is free. The disadvantage is that the solar cells produce electricity only when they absorb light energy.

Revision questions

1 **a)** Explain three safety features of a three-pin plug. [3]

   b) Suggest one reason why an earth wire has low resistance. [1]   **[4 marks]**

2 The table below shows how the number of cells in a battery affects voltage and current.

Number of cells	Voltage/V	Current/A
1	2	0.2
2	4	0.3
3	6	0.4
4	8	0.5

   a) Give one trend shown by these results. [1]

   b) Using the equation power = voltage × current, calculate the power used in watts when the battery has four cells. [1]   **[2 marks]**

3 **a)** Explain how electricity is generated. [2]

   b) Describe the role of a turbine in a fossil-fuel power station. [2]   **[4 marks]**

4 Calculate the cost of using an electric fire with a power 3500 W for one day if the cost of electricity is 15 pence per kWh.   **[3 marks]**

5 **a)** In the diagram below what is represented by **X** and **Y**? [2]

power station   240V to homes

   b) Describe and explain the function of a step-up transformer. [3]   **[5 marks]**

15 Waves and communication

Waves

Waves are **vibrations** that carry **energy** from one place to another.

Types of waves

There are two types of wave motion.

1 **Longitudinal waves** – the particles vibrate in the **same direction** (are parallel) to the direction of travel. **Sound** travels as longitudinal waves.

In the slinky spring in Figure 15.1, the particles vibrate in the same direction (plane) that the wave is travelling (along the spring).

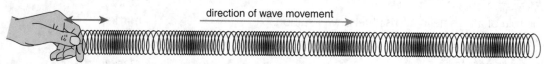

direction of wave movement

hand movement

↑ Figure 15.1 A longitudinal wave

2 **Transverse waves** – the particles vibrate at right angles to the direction that the wave is travelling. **Electromagnetic** waves, including light, are transverse waves.

In the slinky spring in Figure 15.2, the particles vibrate at **right angles** (are perpendicular) to the direction the wave is travelling.

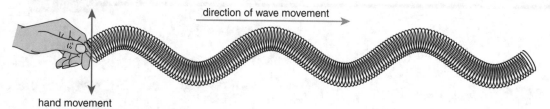

direction of wave movement

hand movement

↑ Figure 15.2 A transverse wave

Features of transverse waves

All waves have three important features – **wavelength**, **frequency** and **amplitude**:

● the wavelength is the distance between two successive crests or troughs

● the amplitude is the maximum height of a wave

● the frequency is the number of waves passing a particular point in one second.

Figure 15.3 shows the wavelength and amplitude of a typical transverse wave.

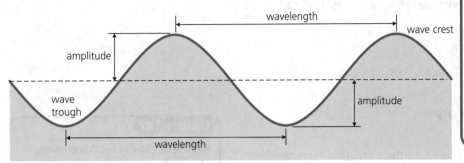

↑ **Figure 15.3 Wavelength and amplitude**

Frequency is measured in **hertz (Hz)** – a wave that has one complete wave passing a particular point each second has a frequency of 1 Hz.

The wave equation

This gives the relationship between speed, frequency and wavelength:

speed = frequency × wavelength

Worked example

Calculate the speed of a wave that has a wavelength of 5 cm and a frequency of 2 Hz.

Answer

speed = frequency × wavelength
     = 2 × 5
     = 10 cm/s

Exam tip

Diagrams similar to Figure 15.3 appear in exam papers often. Many candidates incorrectly measure amplitude as the distance from the wave trough to the wave crest – they double the correct value.

Exam tip

Wavelength and amplitude can be measured in metres (m), centimetres (cm) or millimetres (mm).

Sound   Revised ☐

Sound has the following features:

● it is a longitudinal wave

● it is produced by vibrating objects that cause the air to vibrate

● it cannot travel through a vacuum

● bigger vibrations → bigger amplitudes → louder sounds.

Hearing

The **audible hearing range** covers the frequencies that humans can hear. The audible hearing range is **from 20 Hz to 20 kHz**. Many older people find it difficult to hear sounds over a frequency of 14 kHz.

Common reasons why some people find it hard to hear include:

● age

● ear damage – such as to the eardrum

● defects from birth

● being subjected to loud noises for too long – for example at work or at venues with loud music.

Ultrasound

Ultrasound has a frequency **higher than 20 kHz**. Ultrasound cannot be heard by humans.

Ultrasound has many uses including:

- **foetal scanning** – checking the health and size of a foetus in the womb
- checking for problems in **body organs** – for example looking for gallstones
- **measuring distances** – ultrasound scanners are used by estate agents to quickly and accurately measure room sizes; boats use ultrasound to calculate the depth of water or to find shoals of fish.

Echoes

An **echo** is a reflected sound. Hard surfaces **reflect** most of the sound that hits them; soft surfaces **absorb** most of the sound and reflect less.

You will see later how echoes can be useful, but sometimes they are not. Echoes can create problems in concert halls and reduce the quality of music. To reduce echoes, many concert halls (auditoria) have soft furnishings such as curtains and carpets, covering the walls and floors. These furnishings absorb rather than reflect sound.

Measuring the speed of sound

The speed of sound can be measured in different ways.

The echo method

1 Two students stand together, some distance away from a hard structure like a wall or building.

2 One student bangs two wooden blocks together.

3 The other uses a stopwatch to measure the time between hearing the original bang and hearing its echo.

4 The speed of sound can be calculated using the equation:

$$\text{speed} = \frac{\text{distance}}{\text{time}}$$

Worked example

Two students carried out an investigation to measure the speed of sound using the echo method described above. The wall was 290 metres away and the average time between the initial sound and the echo was 2 seconds.

a) Calculate the speed of sound using the formula $\text{speed} = \dfrac{\text{distance}}{\text{time}}$

b) The speed of sound in air is normally 330 m/s. Suggest one reason why the students' value was slightly different from this.

Answer

a) $\text{speed} = \dfrac{580\,\text{m (distance to the wall and back)}}{2\text{ seconds}} = 290\,\text{m/s}$

b) Slow reactions of the time keeper.

The flash–bang method

This method does not involve echoes – it involves two people who are a considerable distance apart, for example 1 kilometre. One of the people is in a car and the other (the recorder) is a considerable distance away with a stopwatch.

1 The person in the car flashes the headlights and sounds the horn at the same time.

2 Immediately the lights are seen by the other person, the stopwatch is started.

3 Once the sound is heard, the stopwatch is stopped.

4 The person in the car and the recorder change positions (to cancel out wind effects) and the process is repeated.

5 Several readings can be taken in each position to improve reliability.

6 The speed of sound is calculated using the formula $\text{speed} = \dfrac{\text{distance}}{\text{time}}$

Exam tip

When describing the flash–bang method, it is important to state that the car and the person with the stopwatch are a large distance apart – at least 1 kilometre. Otherwise the time difference between seeing the lights and hearing the horn is too short to measure accurately.

↑ Figure 15.4 The flash-bang method of measuring the speed of sound

The electromagnetic spectrum

Revised

The **electromagnetic spectrum** is the range of electromagnetic waves. They range from very short wave gamma radiation (about 0.000 000 000 01 m) to long wave radio waves (about 1000 m).

gamma rays	X-rays	ultraviolet (UV)	visible light	infrared (IR)	microwaves	radio waves

← increasing frequency : increasing wavelength →

All electromagnetic waves:

● carry energy

● travel as transverse waves

● travel at the same speed through a vacuum.

Effects of electromagnetic waves on living cells

Some types of electromagnetic waves can harm living cells (living tissue).

● Too much UV radiation can cause skin cancer.

● X-rays can damage or kill cells and cause cancer

● Gamma rays can also damage or kill cells and cause cancer.

The table on page 105 shows that while wavelength increases from left to right, frequency increases from right to left across the range of electromagnetic waves. The waves become increasingly dangerous to human cells as their **frequency increases** and they have **more energy** i.e. gamma rays are the most harmful to living cells.

How do microwaves heat food?

Microwaves cause the water molecules in food to absorb energy – this causes them to **vibrate more**. This rapid movement of the water molecules causes the temperature of the food to rise. Because of their effect on water molecules, microwave heating is particularly effective for foods that contain a lot of water.

Exam tip

Moving to the left in the spectrum, the frequency and energy increase. This explains why gamma radiation and X-rays can penetrate living tissue but UV radiation damages cells only in the skin.

Communications and electromagnetic waves

Revised

Electromagnetic waves are very important in communicating information – as shown in the table.

Electromagnetic wave	Use
radio waves	television and radio
microwaves	satellite and mobile phones
infrared	telephone networks using optical fibres/ TV remote controls
visible light	telephone networks using optical fibres

Telephone messages can be sent along copper wire (the older traditional method).

Optical fibres are better (than copper wire) for a number of reasons. These include:

● optical fibres carry more information

● the signals do not need to be boosted as often

● there will be less interference.

Mobile phones

Mobile phones send and receive messages by **microwaves**. The signal from a mobile phone is sent to the nearest communications mast. From there the signal is sent through a series of masts that act as **repeater stations** until the signal reaches the receiver. The area serviced by a particular mast is called a **cell**.

Exam tip

If a series of masts (repeater stations) was not used, the signals would need to be much stronger. To get a stronger signal, phones would need to be much larger.

a   b

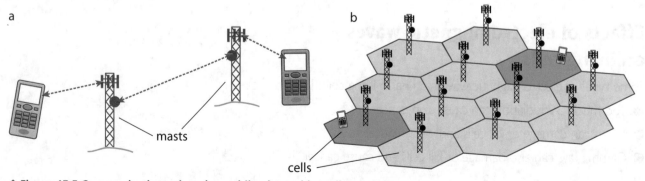

masts

cells

↑ **Figure 15.5 Communicating using a) a mobile phone; b) a cell network**

There are health risks involved in using mobile phones. It has been suggested that the microwaves that come from mobile phones and masts can cause harm, particularly cancer.

It is suggested that mobile phones are particularly dangerous for young children because their brain is not fully developed.

Sensible precautions include:

● use headsets or speaker phones – this allows the phone to be kept well away from the head

● do not use mobile phones for long calls (use a landline more often or text)

● siting masts well away from housing areas.

Revision questions

1 The diagram below shows some sea waves.

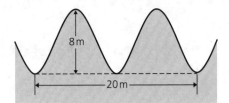

   a) What is the amplitude of these waves? [1]

   b) What is their wavelength? [1]

   c) If five complete waves pass a fixed point in 10 seconds, what is the frequency of these waves? [2]

   d) What is the unit of frequency? [1]

   e) Sea waves are transverse waves – describe a transverse wave. [2] **[7 marks]**

2 Ultrasound travels at 1500 m/s in water. A ship sends out an ultrasound pulse towards the seabed and the echo returns 5 seconds later.

   a) Calculate the depth of the water below the ship. [2]

   b) Suggest **one** explanation for the pulse unexpectedly returning after 2 seconds. [1]

   c) The ultrasound used has a frequency of 25 000 Hz. Use the wave equation speed = frequency × wavelength to calculate the wavelength of this ultrasound. [3] **[6 marks]**

3 The diagram below shows part of the electromagnetic spectrum.

gamma rays	X-rays		visible light		microwaves	radio waves

   a) Copy the diagram and add the two missing types of electromagnetic radiation. [2]

   b) Give **one** thing that all types of electromagnetic radiation have in common. [1]

   c) Give **one** harmful effect of gamma radiation. [1] **[4 marks]**

4 Explain how mobile phone messages travel from person to person. **[3 marks]**

Go online for the answers

GCSE Science Single Award for CCEA 107

16 Vision

Lenses and the eye

Visible light is the part of the electromagnetic spectrum that humans can see. Light travels in straight lines but can change direction by bending as it passes through lenses – the bending of light by a lens is called **refraction**.

Converging and diverging lenses

Converging lenses are thicker in the middle (rather than the edges). These **convex** lenses refract light rays and bring the rays closer together – the rays **converge**.

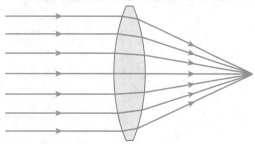

↑ **Figure 16.1 Converging lenses cause light rays to converge**

Diverging lenses are thinner in the middle (rather than the edges). Diverging (or **concave**) lenses refract light rays by bending rays outwards – the rays **diverge**.

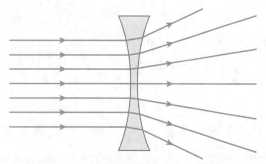

↑ **Figure 16.2 Diverging lenses cause light rays to diverge**

The human eye

The human eye is adapted for sight. The main parts include:

● the **cornea** – an outer transparent layer that converges light rays (most refraction takes place here)

● the **lens** – is convex and further converges light rays and focuses them on the retina. The lens is able to change thickness to provide more or less refraction depending on the angle of light rays reaching the eye

● the **retina** – the sensitive layer at the back of the eye that contains the light-sensitive cells.

Figure 16.3 represents the human eye.

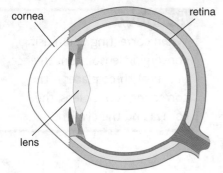

cornea

retina

lens

↑ Figure 16.3 The human eye

Worked example

Describe the passage of light through the eye.

Answer

Light is refracted by the cornea as it enters the eye. Further refraction takes place in the lens. The light rays are focused on the retina.

Eye problems
Revised

Many people find it difficult to see without contact lenses or glasses. The two common eyesight problems, and methods of correction, are described here.

Long sight and its correction

The problem – with long sight, you can see distant objects clearly but close-up objects are blurred.

The reason – light rays from a distant object arrive as parallel rays and need only a small amount of refraction to focus them on the retina. Rays from close-up objects are diverging when they reach the cornea so they need a lot of refraction to be focused. In people with long sight, the eye lens is too weak to provide the additional refraction needed when viewing close-up objects, so the **focal point is behind the retina** – therefore the image is **blurred**.

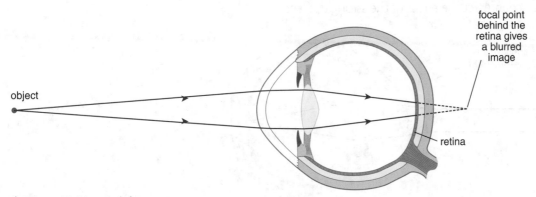

object

focal point behind the retina gives a blurred image

retina

↑ Figure 16.4 Long sight

The correction – for long sight, a **converging** (convex) lens is placed in front of the eye (as glasses or contact lenses). This gives the extra convergence required when viewing a close-up object.

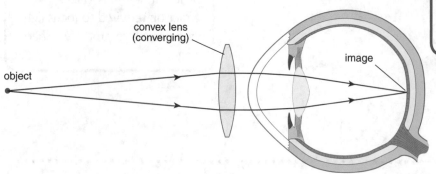

↑ Figure 16.5 The correction of long sight

Short sight and its correction

The problem – with short sight you can see close-up objects clearly but distant objects are blurred.

The reason – the eye lens is too strong so parallel light rays coming from a distant object are converged too much so the **focal point is in front of the retina**. People with short sight can see close-up objects clearly because light rays coming from close-up objects are diverging so need more convergence to focus on the retina – the strong lens is ideal for this role.

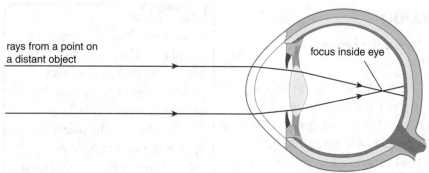

↑ Figure 16.6 Short sight

The correction – a **diverging** (concave) lens is placed in front of the eye to diverge light rays to counteract the effect of the strong eye lens.

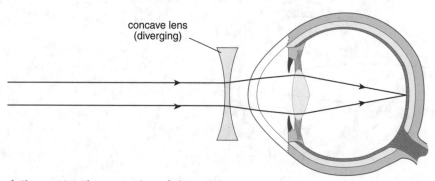

↑ Figure 16.7 The correction of short sight

1   Describe what a converging lens does to parallel rays of light.   **[2 marks]**

2   Describe the role of refraction in focusing light on the human retina.   **[3 marks]**

3   The diagram below shows the eye of someone with an eye defect.

    a) Describe the eye problem shown. [2]

    b) Name the eye problem shown. [1]

    c) Describe how this problem can be corrected. [1]   **[4 marks]**

4   **a)** Describe the cause of short sight. [1]

    b) Describe the effect of short sight. [1]

    c) Explain how short sight is corrected. [1]   **[3 marks]**

Go online for the answers ⟨Online⟩

17 Energy

The most common fuels used today are fossil fuels.

Fossil fuels

Revised

Fossil fuels are the remains of plants and animals that have been compressed (subjected to pressure) by layers of rock for millions of years. The most common fossil fuels are **coal**, **oil** and **natural gas**.

Fossil fuels are **non-renewable** so reserves are finite – they will run out. When burned, they produce carbon dioxide which contributes to **global warming**.

Conserving fossil fuels

Revised

It is important to conserve resources of fossil fuels and also to use energy efficiently.

There are a number of ways in which we can do this.

Using renewable energy sources

We can get more of our electricity from renewable sources. These include:

- solar
- hydroelectric
- tidal
- wave.

Using fuels efficiently

The efficiency of an appliance/device indicates how good it is at transferring energy from one form to another.

The efficiency is calculated using the equation:

$$\text{efficiency} = \frac{\text{useful energy output}}{\text{total energy input}}$$

To be efficient it is important that the useful energy output is nearly the same as the total energy input.

> **Exam tip**
>
> Many questions about efficiency ask you to calculate an efficiency as a percentage. If the device is efficient, its efficiency can approach 100% but it can *never* exceed 100%.

Developing alternative fuels for transport

There is an increasing number of schemes.

- **Biofuel** (**biodiesel**) can be produced from vegetable oil – for example, the oil in the seeds of oilseed rape can be used.
- **Gasohol** is produced by adding alcohol to gas – the alcohol can be made from a range of crops including sugar beet, sugar cane, barley and potatoes. Substances that are used instead of petrol or diesel are called **substitutes** – fuels such as biodiesel/biofuel. Substances that are used together with petrol or diesel are **extenders** – fuels such as the alcohol in gasohol.

- **Regenerative hybrid systems** – in the Toyota Prius and some other modern cars, the high-voltage rechargeable battery is recharged by kinetic energy from the engine. This can be so effective that the battery can remain charged and be used to power the vehicle (and save petrol). In regenerative braking systems the kinetic energy of braking is converted to electricity by generators attached to the wheels – the electricity is used to recharge the battery.

- **Fuel cells** – fuel cells are a special type of battery that can have ingredients added (rather than the battery being recharged). There are many types of fuel that can be used in fuel cells – they include **methanol**. The alcohol needed to make methanol can be obtained from renewable biomass. In a fuel cell the methanol 'reacts' to produce electricity which powers the car.

Another type of fuel cell uses **hydrogen** as the fuel. The cell is used to produce the electricity that powers the car. A big advantage is that there is no shortage of hydrogen and its use does not pollute the atmosphere because it does not produce carbon dioxide – it releases heat and water as by-products.

Methanol and hydrogen are examples of fuel substitutes because they replace petrol or diesel.

Exam tip

Hybrid cars are powered by electricity (from a battery or fuel cell) and petrol or diesel.

Exam tip

There are many other features of modern cars that conserve fuel – stop–start technology, cars made from lightweight materials, better streamlining and so on.

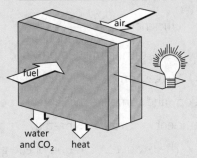
↑ **Figure 17.1 A methanol fuel cell**

Worked example

a) Give one advantage of using fuel cells in cars.

b) Describe and explain one advantage of using hydrogen fuel cells compared to methanol fuel cells.

Answer

a) The fuel used is renewable/not in short supply.

b) Hydrogen does not produce carbon dioxide, so has no effect on global warming.

Conservation of energy
Revised

The Law of the Conservation of Energy states that:

Energy cannot be created or destroyed – it can only be transformed from one form to another.

Take two common examples. All the electrical energy entering a television is used. Only some electrical energy is transferred to useful visible light (the picture) and sound. Some is lost as heat – in efficient modern TVs very little may be lost as heat. However, all the electrical energy entering the TV is converted into one form or another. All the useful energy and wasted energy are eventually transferred to the surroundings, which become warmer.

The energy used in heating some soup in a microwave oven makes the food warmer (useful energy) and some evaporates the water in the soup turning it to steam (waste energy). Eventually all the energy is transferred to the surroundings heating up the person eating the soup and the air.

1 **a)** Explain how fossil fuels are formed. [3]

   b) Give two reasons why it is better to reduce reliance on fossil fuels. [2]   **[5 marks]**

2 The table below gives information about two types of light bulbs.

	Standard filament bulb	Low-energy bulb
Electrical power input	40 W	12 W
Light power output	4 W	4 W
Efficiency/%	0.10	

   a) Calculate the efficiency of the low-energy bulb using the equation: [2]

   $$\text{efficiency} = \frac{\text{power output}}{\text{power input}}$$

   b) Using the information provided, fully explain **one** reason for using low-energy bulbs. [2]

   c) Suggest **one** way in which filament bulbs waste energy. [1]   **[5 marks]**

3 Copy and complete the sentence below. Choose words from:

   efficient   created   heated   transformed   destroyed

   The law of conservation of energy states that energy cannot be _____ or _____;
   it can only be _____ from one form to another.   **[3 marks]**

Go online for the answers Online

18 Transport and road safety

Motor vehicles must be able to stop within the available distance in front of them, otherwise a collision occurs.

Stopping a motor vehicle

Revised

Stopping distance has two parts – thinking distance and braking distance.

- **stopping distance** – the distance travelled between starting to think about stopping and reaching a complete stop
- **thinking distance** – how far the vehicle travels while the driver is thinking about what to do
- **braking distance** – how far the vehicle travels after the brakes are activated until reaching a complete stop

  stopping distance = thinking distance + braking distance

Thinking distance and braking distance (and therefore stopping distance) are increased by many factors as shown in the table below.

> **Exam tip**
>
> A thinking distance is measured in metres (or some other unit of distance) not seconds!

Factors that increase thinking distance	Factors that increase braking distance
• faster speed of the vehicle • taking alcohol, drugs and medicines • tiredness	• faster speed of the vehicle • poor brakes • icy or wet weather conditions • bald tyres
the factors above increase the distance travelled while thinking about what to do	the last two bullet points above increase the distance required to brake because they reduce friction between the tyres and the road

> **Exam tip**
>
> If either (or both) the thinking or braking distance increases then the stopping distance increases.

Reaction time

Thinking distance is affected by a driver's **reaction time**. If the reaction time is short, the thinking distance is less. Reaction time is the time that it takes someone to react to a situation – such as a driver reacting to a dog running out in front of the car. It is the time between seeing the dog and starting to do something about it.

Reaction time can be measured using a metre rule as shown in Figure 18.1.

The steps are as follows.

1 Person **A** holds the metre rule by the tip so that it hangs vertically downwards.

2 Person **B** holds an outstretched hand against the bottom end of the metre rule in a grasping position, but not actually holding the rule.

3 Person **A** lets go of the metre rule and **B** catches it as soon as possible.

4 The distance the rule falls before being caught gives an indication of **B**'s reaction time – the longer the distance, the longer the reaction time (and slower the reaction).

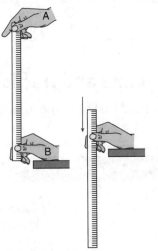

↑ **Figure 18.1 Measuring reaction time**

Friction

Braking distance depends on friction. **Friction** is a force that opposes motion – it is measured in newtons (N).

← friction   motion →

↑ **Figure 18.2 Friction opposes motion**

Friction is produced when two surfaces, like the tyres and the road, rub together. Factors that affect friction include:

● the heavier the weight (e.g. of a car), the higher the friction

● the rougher the surface, the higher friction – this explains why tyres have more friction on a dry road than on an icy road.

Road safety

Revised

There are many safety features to improve road safety.

Safety in cars

Safety feature	Function
seat belts	restrain the driver and passengers preventing them being thrown forward on impact
airbags	the shock of impact causes airbags to inflate rapidly providing a cushion between the driver (and passengers) and the steering wheel and other hard surfaces
crumple zones	situated at the front and rear of cars and on impact absorb energy as they 'crumple' and collapse slowly – this reduces the force that people inside the car are subjected to
rigid passenger cells	the cabin that encloses the driver and passengers is tough and rigid – it will normally not collapse on impact protecting those inside from crush injuries

Speed limits and traffic-calming measures

Speed limits and traffic-calming measures are other methods used to promote road safety.

Feature	Description	Function
speed limits	these are the upper speed limits set by the Government – the limits are different for different types of road: in a built-up area it is typically 30 mph but for motorways it is 70 mph	speed limits make accidents less likely and reduce the extent of injury if an accident occurs
speed bumps	slow vehicles down in built-up areas – if drivers go over bumps too quickly they can damage their vehicles	accidents are less likely and reduce the extent of injury if an accident happens
other traffic-calming measures	road-narrowing schemes are designed to slow traffic down	accidents are less likely and reduce the extent of injury

Speed cameras can identify speeding vehicles. Speeding drivers (identified by their vehicle's registration number) can be fined and/or have penalty points added to their licences.

There are two types of speed camera and they measure speed in different ways.

● **Instantaneous speed** is the speed at a particular moment in time – such as the speed at the actual time a traffic camera takes a picture.

● **Average speed** is the average speed that a car is travelling at over a set distance – to measure average speed at least two cameras at different places along a road are required; these calculate the average speed by measuring the time taken for a vehicle to travel a particular distance.

Speed

Revised ☐

'Speed' tells us how quickly something is travelling. For example, a car could have a speed of 45 miles per hour (mph). This tells you it will travel 45 miles (distance) in 1 hour (time).

$$\text{average speed} = \frac{\text{total distance travelled}}{\text{total time taken}}$$

Distance–time graphs

A **distance–time graph** is a graph of distance (on the *y*-axis) against time (on the *x*-axis).

Key points in interpreting distance–time graphs are:

● a straight diagonal line means the object (e.g. car) is moving at a constant speed

● the steeper the diagonal line, the faster the speed

● horizontal lines mean the object is not moving (speed = 0).

Worked example

Figure 18.3 shows a distance–time graph for a car over a period of 60 seconds.

a) Use the graph to find the distance the car travels in the first 15 seconds.

b) Between which two letters is the car changing its speed most quickly?

c) Calculate the total time for which the car was stopped.

d) Use the equation

$$\text{average speed} = \frac{\text{total distance travelled}}{\text{total time taken}}$$

to calculate the average speed over the 60 seconds.

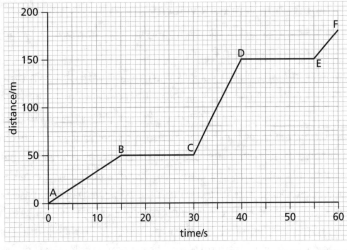

↑ Figure 18.3

Answer

a) 50 m

b) **C–D** (steepest angle)

c) **(B–C)** + **(D–E)** = (30 − 15) + (55 − 40) = 30 s

d) $\frac{180}{60}$ = 3 m/s

Using a data logger to measure speed

Figure 18.4 shows how a data logger can be used to measure the speed of a moving trolley.

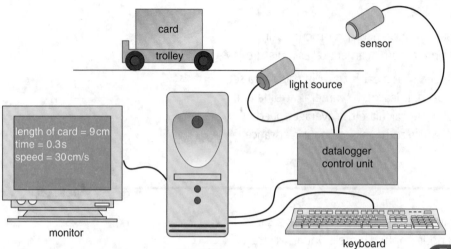

length of card = 9 cm
time = 0.3 s
speed = 30 cm/s

↑ **Figure 18.4 Measuring the speed of a trolley**

- The card on the trolley breaks the beam of light and triggers the timer on as the card starts passing through it.

- When the back of card travels past the sensor, the beam is restored and triggers the timer off.

- The computer asks for the length of the card and you enter this using the keyboard.

- The computer uses speed = $\dfrac{\text{distance}}{\text{time}}$ to work out the average speed.

Exam tip

You could be asked to describe how you could investigate how the slope of a ramp affects the speed of a trolley. You could use a data logger as above and increase/decrease the height of the ramp in steps. You would need to keep other variables (such as the surface on the ramp and the trolley used) constant.

Momentum

Revised

Moving objects have **momentum** – this is calculated using the equation:

momentum = mass × velocity

If mass is measured in kilograms and velocity in metres per second, then momentum is given in **kg m/s**.

When a moving object collides with a stationary object, momentum is transferred from the moving object to the stationary one. This transfer of momentum causes the objects to exert a force on each other.

The longer it takes for the momentum to be transferred, the smaller is the force at any one time. Use is made of this by using crumple zones and airbags in motor cars. If a car is involved in a collision, the passengers are protected better because the crumple zones/airbags increase the length of time the force is acting for during the collision – this reduces the forces on the passengers and reduces their momentum change in the collision. The time may be only a few milliseconds but they make a big difference.

Exam tip

'Velocity' is similar to 'speed' – it is measured in m/s.

Balanced and unbalanced forces

Several forces can act on an object at any one time – for a moving car, friction with the road and the air opposing motion, the force of the engine promoting forward motion and gravity providing a downwards force.

There are some key features about combined forces and motion:

● If the forces are equal in size but opposite in direction, they are balanced.

● If the forces are balanced, an object will either remain at rest or move in a straight line with a constant speed.

● If the forces are unbalanced, the resultant force causes the object to accelerate/decelerate and/or change direction.

Worked example

A car has a forward force of 1200 N and a backward force of 1000 N. Describe, in terms of the resultant force, the motion of the car.

Answer

The resultant force is 1200 − 1000 = 200 N forwards. The car accelerates in the forward direction.

Revision questions

Tested

1 The table below shows some information about the stopping distance of a car at different speeds.

Speed/mph	Thinking distance/m	Braking distance/m	Stopping distance/m
25	7	14	21
50	15	40	
75		80	104

a) Complete the table by calculating the **two** missing values. [2]

b) Describe the relationship between speed and stopping distance. [1]

c) Apart from speed, state **two** factors that affect braking distance. [2]   **[5 marks]**

2 a) State **two** features of modern cars that are designed to reduce passenger injuries if a car is involved in a collision. [2]

b) i) Describe how speed bumps promote driver and passenger safety. [2]

ii) Suggest **one** disadvantage of speed bumps. [1]   **[5 marks]**

3 The graph shows a distance–time graph for two bicycles (**A** and **B**) travelling along a road.

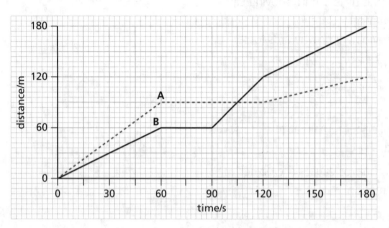

a) How far had bicycle **A** travelled after 60 seconds? [1]

b) Which bicycle travelled furthest over 180 seconds? [1]

c) Which bicycle was stopped for the longest time? Explain your answer. [3]

d) Use the equation:

$$\text{average speed} = \frac{\text{total distance travelled}}{\text{total time taken}}$$

to calculate the average speed for bicycle **A** over the entire journey. [2]   **[7 marks]**

4 A cyclist of mass 50 kg travelled at a velocity of 20 m/s on a bicycle of mass 15 kg.

Use the equation:

momentum = mass × velocity

to calculate the total momentum of the cyclist and the bicycle.
Your answer should include the appropriate units.   **[3 marks]**

5 a) A car is moving in a straight line driven by a resultant force of 5000 N. The total frictional force is 10 000 N. Calculate the forward force produced by the engine. [2]

b) i) Describe the overall effect these forces are having on the car. [1]

ii) State one way in which the driver can make the forces balanced. [1]   **[4 marks]**

Go online for the answers   Online

19 Radioactivity

Atoms and radiation Revised

Matter is made up of very tiny particles called **atoms**. Inside each atom there are three types of small (subatomic) particles – **protons**, **neutrons** and **electrons**.

The properties of these particles are shown in the table.

Particle	Position	Relative mass	Relative charge
proton	nucleus	1	+1
neutron	nucleus	1	0
electron	shells outside nucleus	negligible	−1

Radioactive elements have atoms that have unstable nuclei because of unstable combinations of protons and neutrons. These unstable atoms:

● disintegrate or decay (split up)

● form smaller, more stable atoms

● they emit radiation as this happens.

Types of radiation

There are three types of radiation that can be emitted from radioactive nuclei.

Type	Description	Stopped by	Charge
alpha (α)	• large, heavy, slow particles • helium atom that has lost its two electrons	• a few centimetres of air • a sheet of paper	+2
beta (β)	• small, light and fast-moving electrons	• a few metres of air • a few millimetres of aluminium	−1
gamma (γ)	• fast and powerful electromagnetic radiation	• a few centimetres of lead	0

Background radiation

Background radiation is radiation that is all around us – it is always present. Like other radiation, background radiation is caused by the disintegration of unstable nuclei.

Sources of background radiation include:

● **radon** – a radioactive gas emitted from granite rocks

● **carbon-14** – a type of carbon found inside living organisms

● **cosmic rays** reaching the Earth from space

● **nuclear reactors** in nuclear power stations.

> **Exam tip**
>
> You have met gamma radiation before – it is part of the electromagnetic spectrum. You need to be aware that it has high energy and is very dangerous.

> **Exam tip**
>
> In exam questions, 'background radiation' is often the explanation used to account for graphs showing the amount of radiation levelling off but not reaching zero.

Half-life

In a radioactive element, atoms decay and disintegrate – so the number of atoms of that radioactive element must decrease with time.

The **half-life** is the length of time it takes for half of the atoms in a radioactive sample to disintegrate. In effect, the level of radioactivity falls by half. Figure 19.1 shows what happens during a period of three half-lives of a radioactive element.

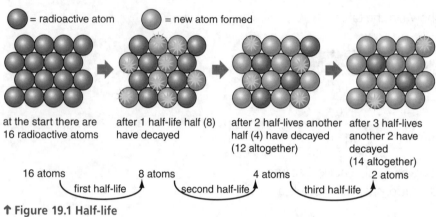

= radioactive atom   = new atom formed

| at the start there are 16 radioactive atoms | after 1 half-life half (8) have decayed | after 2 half-lives another half (4) have decayed (12 altogether) | after 3 half-lives another 2 have decayed (14 altogether) |

16 atoms   8 atoms   4 atoms   2 atoms

first half-life   second half-life   third half-life

↑ **Figure 19.1 Half-life**

Half-life can be represented in graphs as shown in Figure 19.2.

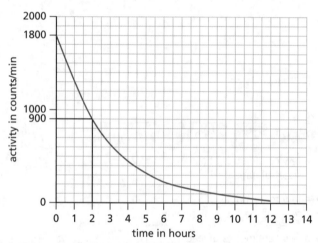

↑ **Figure 19.2 Calculating half-life from a graph**

In Figure 19.2 it takes 2 hours for the activity (level of radiation) to fall from 1800 counts/minute to 900 counts/minute. Therefore the half-life of this element is 2 hours. Similarly after 4 hours the activity is 450 counts/minute and so on.

Worked example

A radioactive element gives a reading of 80 counts/minute. Two hours later the reading was 20 counts/minute. What is the element's half-life?

Answer

1 hour; 20 is a quarter of 80 (after one half-life the value fell to 40, and then to 20 after the second half-life) – so two hours represents 2 half-lives.

Radiation is harmful to living cells. So elements that have short half-lives are usually safer because their level of radioactivity falls more quickly. In general, 'becoming safe' means reaching the background radiation level.

The dangers and benefits of ionising radiation Revised

You need to have some idea of what is meant by the term 'ionising radiation'.

Ionising radiation

(Normal) atoms are electrically neutral because they have equal numbers of (positive) protons and (negative) electrons. When alpha, beta or gamma radiation collide with atoms they tend to displace electrons from their shells – the atoms become positively charged because they now have more protons than electrons.

These charged atoms are now **ions** – the process of turning electrically neutral atoms into ions is called **ionisation**. Alpha and beta particles and gamma radiation are called **ionising radiations** because they cause ionisation.

Harmful effects and uses of ionising radiation

When human body cells are ionised by radiation some cells can be killed or the radiation can cause **cancer**.

However, gamma radiation can also be used in medicine (**radiotherapy**) to kill cancer cells. The amount of radiation (dose) must be accurate and strong enough to kill the cancer cells but not harm healthy cells.

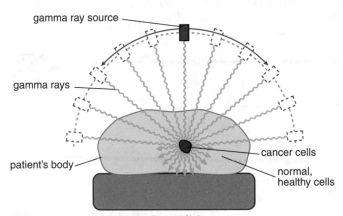

↑ **Figure 19.3 Gamma rays in medicine**

Gamma rays can also be used to:

● **sterilise** surgical instruments by killing any microorganisms (bacteria, fungi or viruses)

● **preserve** (extend the shelf-life) of perishable fresh food by killing microorganisms and stopping decay.

Exam tip

Ionisation radiation damages or kills cells – their harmful effects *and* uses depend on this fact.

1 Explain why some elements are radioactive. **[2 marks]**

2 **a)** Explain what is meant by 'background radiation'. [1]

  b) Give **one** source of background radiation. [1] **[2 marks]**

3 The activity of a radioactive isotope changes as shown in the table.

Time/days	Activity/cpm
0	440
1	330
2	220
3	165
4	110
5	82

  a) Describe the trend shown by the table. [1]

  b) What is the half-life of the isotope? [1] **[2 marks]**

4 A radioactive source and a radioactive detector are placed as shown in the diagram.

radioactive
source

detector

  a) Describe how you could determine whether the radioactive source emits alpha, beta or gamma radiation. [4]

  b) State **two** things that would have to be kept the same to make the results valid. [2]

  c) State why the count never reaches zero. [1] **[7 marks]**

5 **a)** Explain why gamma radiation is a suitable source for treating cancer in the body. [2]

  b) Give one other use for gamma radiation. [1] **[3 marks]**

Go online for the answers

Online

20 The Earth in space

The Solar System

Our Solar System has one **star** (the Sun) surrounded by eight **planets** that travel in paths called **orbits**.

Figure 20.1 shows the Sun, the eight planets and their orbits.

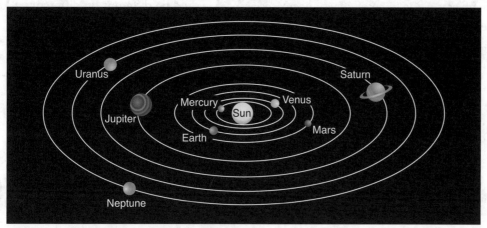

↑ **Figure 20.1 The Solar System (not to scale)**

There are some key points about the Solar System:

- all the planets travel around the Sun in the same direction
- the further a planet is from the Sun, the longer it takes to orbit it
- the planets further from the Sun have elliptical (oval-shaped) orbits – those closer have more circular orbits.

Some of the other structures in the Solar System are listed below.

- **Comets** are formed from rock covered by frozen water and frozen gases – these orbit the Sun.

- **Asteroids** are large chunks of rock that also orbit the Sun – most asteroids are found in a zone (the asteroid belt) between Mars and Jupiter. Occasionally, an asteroid can be knocked out of its orbit and come close to the Earth. Collisions between asteroids and the Earth are possible and have happened in the past – evidence includes the existence of large **craters** caused by such impacts.

- **Moons** orbit planets – the Earth has one moon; there are 173 moons altogether around the planets in the Solar System.

> **Exam tip**
>
> You need to know the order of the planets moving away from the Sun – they are Mercury, Venus, Earth, Mars, Jupiter, Saturn, Uranus and Neptune.

> **Exam tip**
>
> You should also be aware that the further a planet is from the Sun, the colder it is likely to be.

Models of the Solar System

In the **geocentric model**, early humans assumed that the Sun and the other planets orbited the Earth – they thought that the Earth was the centre of the Solar System. As scientific knowledge increased, this was proved to be wrong. Problems included the knowledge that the orbits of the planets were not consistent with the Earth being the centre of the Solar System – for example sometimes Venus appears closer to the Earth than Mars; at other times Mars is closer than Venus. This could not happen if the Earth was the centre. It turned out that scientists had not discovered all the planets so the geocentric model was incomplete.

The **heliocentric model** is the currently accepted model with the Sun at the centre of the Solar System – this model fits all the available evidence.

Gravity and weight

Gravity is the force of attraction that exists between objects. The force depends on:

- the **mass** of the objects – the bigger the objects, the larger the force of gravity
- the **distance** between the objects – the force of gravity decreases as the distance apart increases.

Gravity can be very important – it is the force that keeps us humans on the surface of the Earth – if there was no gravity we would float out into space.

The force of gravity is what causes all objects to have **weight** – this is measured in **newtons per kilogram (N/kg)**.

Exam tip

You should know that your mass will not change wherever you are, but that your weight would be different on different planets. For example, you weigh about six times less on the Moon compared to on Earth. This is because the mass of the Moon is about one-sixth that of the Earth.

Worked example

Explain why astronauts orbiting the Earth can leave their spacecraft and float in space.

Answer

When orbiting the Earth, the effect of the Earth's gravity is reduced because of the large distance away from Earth.

Stars and galaxies

Revised

All **stars** are formed by the same sequence of events.

1 A cloud of **hydrogen** comes together under the force of gravity.

2 As the hydrogen is compressed (pulled together) becoming very dense, its temperature rises to many million degrees.

3 At these extremely high temperatures, **nuclear fusion** reactions occur and the hydrogen nuclei combine to form heavier nuclei such as helium.

4 This nuclear fusion emits light and heat (and other radiation).

Galaxies

A **galaxy** is a huge collection of stars – the galaxy that contains our Solar System is called the **Milky Way**.

The **Universe** is the name given to the space occupied by all the galaxies that exist. These galaxies do not remain settled in the one position in the Universe – they move away from each other.

The distances between stars (and between different galaxies) are so large that we do not use the normal units of measurement, such as kilometres. Distances between stars and galaxies are measured in **light years** – one light year is the distance that light travels in one year.

Exam tip

Remember that a light year is a *distance*, not a *time* – it is approximately 9.3×10^{12} kilometres.

Because of the massive distances involved, space travel between stars poses great difficulties. These include:

- the very large distances and, therefore, times involved – space travellers setting out from one star to another would die before reaching their destination
- the complexities of designing and navigating spacecraft that would need to work for such a long time
- the difficulty in being able to carry enough food, water and oxygen for the travellers.

The expanding Universe
Revised

There are two key features about the movement of galaxies.

- They are continually moving away from each other – and the further away from each other they are, the faster they are moving apart
- As galaxies move apart, space and the Universe are expanding.

Evidence for the galaxies moving apart

All the stars in the Universe emit light in the form of electromagnetic radiation. Analysis of the spectra of this starlight, which ranges from violet to red on the basis of wavelength, shows the presence of black lines (absorption spectrum) where atoms of hydrogen (and other elements) have absorbed some of the light.

When we examine the light spectra from stars in distant galaxies:

- the absorption spectrum pattern is broadly the same across all galaxies
- but it is shifted (in Figure 20.2) towards the red end of the spectrum – this is called red-shift
- the further away a galaxy, the larger the red-shift.

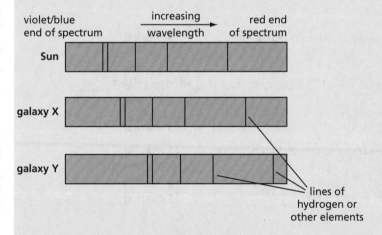

↑ **Figure 20.2 Red-shift in distant galaxies**

The red-shift happens because the light coming from a source that is moving away from us has a longer wavelength than it would have if the source was stationary.

Worked example

Use Figure 20.2 to explain how you know that galaxy **Y** is further away from us than galaxy **X**.

Answer

The light from galaxy **Y** has a bigger red-shift – equivalent lines have moved further to the red end of the spectrum – than the light from galaxy **X**. The bigger the red-shift, the longer the distance.

The origin of the Universe

Most scientists think that the **Big Bang theory** is the best explanation for the origin of the Universe.

It started as a tiny point, called a **singularity**, about **14 billion years ago**. The Big Bang represents a massive cosmic expansion (explosion) that expelled matter and energy in all directions out from this central point. Over millions of years, gravity pulled the scattered matter together to form galaxies, stars, planets and moons. The forces involved are causing the Universe and space to continue to expand – evidence of this is provided by the red-shift of distant galaxies.

There are other theories as to how the Universe began – the best known is the **Steady State theory**. This proposes that the Universe has not changed much throughout time and that it had no significant beginning, such as the Big Bang. It suggests that new matter is continually created as the Universe expands. Most scientists do not support this theory.

Revision questions

Tested

1 Copy and complete the following sentences.

   a) .... are objects that orbit a star. [1]

   b) .... are objects that orbit a planet. [1]

   c) .... contain millions of stars and move away from each other. [1] **[3 marks]**

2 a) Name the planet closest to our Sun. [1]

   b) Explain why the surface temperature of Mars is likely to be warmer than that of Neptune. [1]

   c) What is the name of the currently accepted model of the Solar System? [1] **[3 marks]**

3 Explain fully why a human's weight is less on the Moon than on Earth. **[3 marks]**

4 a) What is meant by the term 'light year'? [2]

   b) Explain why distances in space are measured in light years. [1] **[3 marks]**

5 a) Write the following in order of size, starting with the smallest:

Universe   Solar System   galaxy   star [1]

b) When scientists analyse the light from two distant galaxies they see the following patterns.

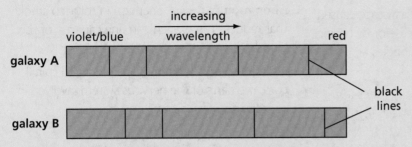

i) What causes the difference in the patterns? [1]

ii) State one conclusion that can be drawn from this information. [1]

iii) Suggest how light coming from the Milky Way would be different from the patterns shown in the diagram. Explain your answer. [3]   **[6 marks]**

Go online for the answers ————————————————————— Online

Biology glossary

Abiotic factor   A non-living factor, e.g. CO_2 level, that can be used to monitor environmental change

Acid rain   Rain that has an acidic pH

Active immunity   Protection against a disease caused by the body recovering from that disease or by having a vaccination. In active immunity, antibodies are produced by the body

Allele   A particular form of a gene. Many genes (e.g. eye colour) can exist in two forms or alleles (e.g. an allele for blue and an allele for brown)

Amino acid   A building block (sub-unit) of proteins

Animal testing   The testing of medicines or drugs on animals

Anorexia   An eating condition caused by eating less than the amount required to maintain weight

Antibiotic   A chemical (medicine) that can kill bacteria (and is therefore effective against most bacterial diseases)

Antibody   A chemical produced by the body to combat microorganisms. Antibody production is stimulated by the presence of antigens in the blood

Antigen   A chemical on the surface of a microorganism, that if present in the body, will cause the production of antibodies

Asexual reproduction   Reproduction involving one parent only

Bacterial resistance (to antibiotics)   Antibiotic-resistant bacteria cannot be killed by antibiotics

Base pairing   The way in which the DNA bases join, i.e. adenine bases join with thymine and cytosine bases join with guanine

Base triplet hypothesis   The idea that sequences of three consecutive bases along a DNA strand code for amino acids

Benedict's test   The test for sugar

Binge drinking   Drinking a lot of alcohol in a short period of time

Biodiversity   The range/number of species in an area

Biotic factor   A living organism, e.g. lichen, that can be used to monitor environmental change

Biuret test   The test for protein

Bulimia   An eating condition in which individuals binge eat then induce vomiting

Cancer   Uncontrolled cell division

Cannabis   An illegal drug that can make users feel relaxed or 'chilled'. There is evidence that its use can lead to mental health problems in some people

Carbon monoxide   A chemical in tobacco smoke that reduces the oxygen-carrying capacity of the blood

Central Nervous System   The brain and spinal cord, the parts of the nervous system involved in coordination

Cervix   The opening to the uterus

Chargaff (Erwin)   The scientist who discovered that the number of adenine bases was the same as the number of thymine bases in DNA (also that the number of guanine bases is the same as cytosine bases)

Cholesterol   A fatty substance that causes narrowing of blood vessels

Chromosome   A genetic structure in the nucleus that is made of DNA. Chromosomes contain sequences of genes

Circulatory disease   A disease that affects the heart and/or blood vessels

Classification   The naming of organisms and their allocation to particular groups

Clinical trial   The testing of a medicine or drug on human volunteers or patients

Cocaine   A very addictive illegal drug that is a stimulant and can give users a 'high'

Collaborative nature of science   The principle that progress in science involves input by many scientists, each building on the work of others

Competitive invasive species   A non-native species (introduced by man) that spreads rapidly, outcompeting native species

Continuous variation   The type of variation in which there is gradual change in a feature with no distinct groups, e.g. height

Contraception   The prevention of pregnancy

Cystic fibrosis   A medical condition caused by the presence of two recessive alleles in a particular gene

Deforestation   The removal of large areas of woodland or forest by man

Diabetes   A condition in which the body is unable to control blood sugar levels

Discontinuous variation   The type of variation in which individuals can be easily allocated to a distinct group with no overlap, e.g. human blood groups

DNA   The core coding component of chromosomes and genes

DNA bases   The bases, adenine, cytosine, guanine and thymine, that provide the genetic code in DNA

DNA code   The arrangement of bases along the coding strand

Double Helix   The structure (arrangement) of DNA

Down syndrome   A condition in which affected individuals have 47 (rather than 46) chromosomes

Effector   A part of the body that can make a response, e.g. muscle

Emulsion test   The test for fat

Endangered species   A species that is at risk of extinction (because there are so few individuals left)

Epidemic   The rapid spread of a disease (e.g. flu) through a town or small region such as Northern Ireland with many people becoming infected

Evolution   The process of change in a species (type of organism) over time

Extinction   A species is extinct if there are no living members of that species left

Food chain   The order in which energy passes through a sequence of living organisms

Food web   A number of interlinked food chains

Franklin (Rosalind) and Wilkins (Maurice)   The scientists who used X-ray diffraction to work out that DNA has a helix shape

Gene   A section of a chromosome that controls a particular characteristic, e.g. eye colour

Gene therapy   The process in which a functional gene is added to an individual to replace a faulty (disease-causing) gene

Genetic engineering   The insertion of DNA obtained from an individual of one species into an individual of a different species

Genetic screening   Testing (often of a foetus) for the presence of a particular genetic condition

Genotype   The symbols representing the two alleles of a gene, e.g. tt

Global warming   The ongoing increase in temperature of the Earth's atmosphere

GM crops (genetically modified crops)   Crops that have been produced by genetic engineering

Heart rate   The number of times the heart beats per minute

Heterozygous   The condition in which the two alleles of a gene are different, e.g. Tt'

Homozygous   The condition in which both alleles of a gene are the same, e.g. TT or tt

Hormones   Chemical messengers that travel in the blood to a target organ, where they act

Inherited disease (condition)   A condition that is passed genetically from parent to child

Insulin   A hormone, produced by the pancreas, that lowers blood sugar levels

In vitro testing   The testing of medicines or drugs on cells in the laboratory

Iodine test   The test for starch

Karyotype A diagram or photograph of all the chromosomes in a cell carefully laid out (usually in pairs) so they can be counted

Menstrual cycle   A monthly (28 day) cycle in human females that prepares the uterus for pregnancy

Microorganism (microbe)   An extremely small organism that can only be seen by using a microscope

MMR   A vaccination programme to combat measles, mumps and rubella

MRSA   A type of bacterium that is resistant to most antibiotics

Mucous membrane   A thin mucus-covered membrane in the body, e.g. the nasal cavity, that traps microorganisms and prevents infection

Mutation   A random change in the structure or number of chromosomes or genes

Natural selection   The natural process in which certain individuals are better adapted, and therefore more likely to survive, than other more poorly-adapted individuals

Nicotine   A chemical in tobacco smoke that is addictive and affects heart rate

Nitrification   The process in the nitrogen cycle in which (nitrifying) bacteria convert ammonia to nitrate

Oestrogen   A female hormone important in the control of the menstrual cycle

Ovary   The part of the female reproductive system that produces the ova (eggs)

Oviduct   The part of the female reproductive system that transports ova (eggs) from the ovary to the uterus (fertilisation occurs in the oviduct)

Palisade cell   A specialised cell adapted for photosynthesis, found near the upper leaf surface

Pandemic The rapid spread of disease on a large scale, e.g. through many countries with many people affected

Passive immunity   Protection against disease due to being given antibodies from another source (not produced by the person getting the antibodies)

Pasteur (Louis) The scientist who showed that contamination could only occur if microorganisms could gain entry

Pedigree diagram   A genetic diagram that shows how a condition or characteristic is inherited through several generations of a family

Peer review   The process in which scientific discoveries are evaluated by other scientists

Penicillin   The first antibiotic. Alexander Fleming was the first person to identify its significance

Penis   The part of the male reproductive system that helps place sperm into the vagina of the female reproductive system

Phagocytosis   The process by which certain white blood cells (phagocytes) engulf and destroy microorganisms in the blood

Phenotype   The outward appearance of the genotype, e.g. tall or short

Photosynthesis   The process by which plants make food using light energy

Phototropism   A plant growth response involving plants growing in the direction of light

Pollution   The addition of substances to the environment in amounts that cause harm

Primary consumer An animal that eats plants

Producer   A plant that makes food by photosynthesis. The first stage in a food chain

Progesterone   A female hormone important in the control of the menstrual cycle

Prostate gland   The part of the male reproductive system that nourishes (feeds) the sperm

Recessive allele   An allele that is masked by a dominant allele. The recessive condition is only shown if two recessive alleles are present

Reflex action   A rapid involuntary action that does not involve conscious thought

Respiration   The process by which living organisms use food to produce energy

Scrotum   The part of the male reproductive system that holds the testes

Secondary (or tertiary) consumer   An animal that eats other animals

Senses   The components of the environment, e.g. sight, that humans are sensitive to

Sexual reproduction   Reproduction that involves two parents. Each parent produces gametes (sex cells) that combine to form the new individual

Side effect   An unwanted or unintended response to taking a drug or medicine

Sperm tube   The part of the male reproductive system that transports sperm from the testes to the urethra

Stroke   A circulatory disease that affects the brain

Sustainable   Behaving in a way that does not harm our environment or significantly deplete its resources

Tar   A chemical in tobacco smoke that can cause cancer, bronchitis and emphysema

Testes   The part of the male reproductive system that makes sperm

Urethra   The part of the male reproductive system that transports sperm out of the body

Uterus   The part of the female reproductive system where the foetus develops

Vaccination   The placing of dead or weakened microorganisms in the bloodstream to stimulate the body's production of antibodies

Vagina   The part of the female reproductive system where sperm are deposited

Voluntary action   An action or response that involves conscious thought

Watson (James) and Crick (Francis)   The scientists who used modelling (built models) to work out the double helix structure of DNA

Chemistry glossary

Acid   A substance with a pH between 1 and 6

Acid indigestion   Discomfort caused by the production of too much hydrochloric acid by the stomach

Alkali (soluble base)   A substance with a pH between 8 and 14

Alkali metal   A metal element from Group 1 in the Periodic Table. The alkali metals become more reactive as you move down the Periodic Table

Alkaline earth metal   A metal element from Group 2 in the Periodic Table

Alkanes   A particular group of hydrocarbon compounds. Methane, ethane, propane and butane are alkanes

Antacid   A substance used to neutralise excess hydrochloric acid in the stomach

Atom   A very small unit of matter. Atoms are made up of three subatomic particles, protons, electrons and neutrons

Atomic number   The number of protons in the nucleus of an atom

Baking powder   Mixture of baking soda (sodium hydrogencarbonate) and tartaric acid

Baking soda   Sodium hydrogencarbonate, which can be used to combat acid indigestion

Base   A substance that will react with an acid producing a salt and water (e.g. hydroxides)

Biodegradable   Material that can be broken down by microorganisms

Burette   A piece of apparatus that can be used to obtain accurate measurements of liquid being used in a reaction

Cullet   The term used to describe small pieces of glass that can be remoulded as part of glass recycling

Composite material   A material that combines the properties of two (or more) other materials to produce a more useful material for a particular function

Compound   A chemical that has two or more different elements chemically joined (bonded) together

Continental drift   The theory that the continents are moving very slowly. The principle of this movement is explained by plate tectonics

Core   The centre of the Earth. The core is very dense and is a mixture of solid and molten rock

Corrosive (hazard symbol)   Identifies a substance that can burn the skin

Covalent compound   A compound formed with covalent bonds. Covalent bonds are formed between non-metal elements that share electrons, e.g. hydrogen and water

Crude oil   A fossil fuel; a liquid mixture containing many different substances that can be separated using fractional distillation

Crust   The outer part of the Earth's structure. The crust is very thin compared to the mantle and the core. It mainly consists of solid rock

Database   A storage system for storing vast quantities of information, e.g. DNA profiles

Deep Time   The idea that the timescales in the formation of the Universe and Earth are so vast they are almost impossible to comprehend

Displacement reaction   If a more reactive metal is added to a salt solution of another metal, the more reactive metal can displace the less reactive metal (in the solution) forming a salt of the more reactive metal

Distillation   The process of evaporating and then condensing a liquid. Can be used to soften permanent hard water

Earthquake   A sudden movement of parts of the Earth's crust, caused by the edges of two tectonic plates moving alongside or against each other

Electrolysis   The process that breaks down compounds using electricity

Electron   A subatomic particle found in an atom. Electrons have a negligible relative mass and a relative charge of −1

Electron arrangement (electronic structure)   The arrangement of electrons in the shells surrounding the nucleus of an atom

Element   A pure chemical substance that is made from one type of atom

Emission spectroscopy   A technique used to identify metal ions. More specific than a flame test

Explosive (hazard symbol)   Identifies a substance that can explode

Fingerprint   The pattern of very fine lines on a person's fingertip. Everybody has a unique fingerprint and there are four types, arch, loop, whorl and composite

Flame test   A test that involves metal ions producing a particular colour when placed in a Bunsen flame. Can be used to identify metals as each metal ion gives a different colour of flame

Flammable (hazard symbol)   Identifies a substance that can catch fire easily

Fossil   The remains of a dead plant or animal that has been preserved in (sedimentary) rock

Fossil fuel   Fuel formed from the remains of plants and animals that have been compressed by layers of rock for millions of years

Fractional distillation   The process used to separate the compounds in crude oil. It involves heating and evaporation and the subsequent condensation of gas back to a liquid

Genetic fingerprint (DNA profile)   The pattern of bands produced when DNA is treated in a particular way. Each person has a unique DNA fingerprint (pattern of bands)

Group   A vertical column in the Periodic Table. The groups are numbered from 1 to 8. The group number gives the number of electrons in the outer shell of atoms of the elements in the group

Halogens   Group 7 in the Periodic Table

Hard water   Water that does not easily form a lather with soap

Hydrocarbon   A compound containing carbon and hydrogen only

Igneous rock   Rock formed as a result of volcanic activity, e.g. granite and basalt

Indicator   An indicator can be used to determine if a substance is acid, neutral or alkali

Ion exchange   A method of softening permanent hard water. The process involves the exchange of the ions that cause hard water (Ca^{2+} and Mg^{2+}) with e.g. sodium ions (Na^+) in an ion exchange column

Ion   A charged particle produced as a result of an atom losing or gaining one or more electrons

Ionic compound   A compound formed from ions. Ionic compounds contain a metal and a non-metal and electrons are transferred between the elements

Lava   The name given to molten magma when it flows down the sides of volcanoes

Limescale deposits (fur)   The build-up of calcium carbonate or magnesium carbonate in kettles or hot water pipes as a result of the thermal decomposition of temporary hard water

Limewater   The test for carbon dioxide. Limewater turns milky/cloudy if carbon dioxide is bubbled through it

Magma   Molten rock in the Earth's mantle

Mantle   The part of the Earth that lies between the core and the crust. It contains solid and molten rock

Mass number   The total number of protons and neutrons in the nucleus of an atom

Mendeleev (Dmitri)   In 1869 Mendeleev updated Newland's model of the Periodic Table. He left gaps for yet to be discovered elements. The current Periodic Table is very similar to Mendeleev's model

Metamorphic rock   Rock formed by the effect of heat and/or pressure on sedimentary or igneous rock, e.g. marble and slate

Mulch   Decomposing garden waste that can be used as compost

Monomer   A small molecule that can be joined together with many other monomers to make a polymer

Nanotechnology   Technology using very small (nano-scale) parts. Nano-scale components range from 1 to 100 nm. 1 nm is 10^{-9} metres

Natural material   A material that can be obtained from living things, e.g. wool, or made without being processed by chemical methods, e.g. granite

Neutralisation   The reaction between an alkali and an acid producing a salt and water. Also refers to the process of using alkali to 'neutralise' the effect of acid, e.g. adding lime to an acidic soil to make it closer to neutral pH

Neutron   A subatomic particle found in the nucleus of an atom. Neutrons have a relative mass of 1 and a relative charge of 0

Newlands (John)   Arranged the elements in the Periodic Table (in 1864) in order of atomic mass. He developed the law of octaves – the idea that every eighth element had similar properties

Noble gases   Group 8 (0) in the Periodic Table. The noble gases are chemically inert (unreactive)

Non-renewable (finite) energy source   A source that will run out because it cannot be replaced

Oxidation   A reaction where an element or compound gains oxygen

Periodic Table   The table that lists the known elements in a logical order. The Periodic Table provides the chemical symbol, atomic number and mass number of each element

Period   A horizontal row in the Periodic Table. The periods are numbered from 1 to 7 starting at the top. The period number gives the number of electron shells surrounding the nucleus of the atoms of the elements in that period

Permanent hardness (in water)   Hardness that cannot be removed by boiling

pH scale   A scale that runs from pH 1 to pH 14. Substances that have a pH of 1 to 6 are acidic; pH 7 is neutral; and pH's 8 to 14 are alkaline

pH sensor (probe)   An electronic device that gives a numerical value when testing for pH

Photochromic   The name given to paints and dyes that change colour when the light intensity changes

Plate tectonics   The term describing the process of the Earth's tectonic plates floating (and moving) on the underlying mantle

Polymer   A large compound produced by the joining together of many small monomers (sub-units) in a process called polymerisation

Polymerisation   The process of joining many monomers together to form polymers

Precipitate   A solid that results when two (liquid) solutions react

Proton   A subatomic particle found in the nucleus of an atom. Protons have a relative mass of 1 and a relative charge of +1

Radiometric dating   The modern method to find the age of rocks. Radiometric dating uses the rate of decay of radioactive isotopes, e.g. potassium, to calculate the age of a particular rock. Radiometric dating indicates that the Earth is 4.5 billion years old

Richter scale   The scale that measures the strength of earthquakes

Reduction   A reaction in which a compound loses oxygen

Sedimentary rock   Rock built up by small rock particles and/or remains of dead plants and animals forming layers of sediment on the Earth's surface. The rock is formed when the sediment is compressed by more layers of sediment being added, e.g. limestone and sandstone

Seismograph   A special graph that gives information concerning the strength and duration of an earthquake

Sherbet   A mixture of sodium hydrogencarbonate, sugar and solid citric acid. When mixed with water produces carbon dioxide that causes a fizzing sensation in the mouth

Smart material   A material that changes its property if exposed to changes in heat or light intensity

Soft water   Water that lathers easily with soap

Synthetic (man-made) material   A material made as a result of chemical processing, e.g. plastic

Temporary hardness (in water)   Hardness that can be removed by boiling

Thermal decomposition   The use of heat to break down a compound

Thermochromic   The term given to paints or dyes that change colour when heated

Thermoplastic plastic   A type of plastic that can be continually remoulded into different shapes by heating, e.g. polythene and PVC

Thermosetting plastic   A type of plastic that cannot be remoulded after initial setting, e.g. Bakelite and epoxy

Toxic (hazard symbol)   Identifies a substance that can cause harm by poisoning

Ussher (James)   The Archbishop who used the number of generations described in the Bible to estimate the age of the Earth. He concluded that the Earth was created in 4004 BC (approximately 6000 years ago)

Volcano   A landform in an area of weakness where molten magma from the Earth's mantle reaches the Earth's surface

Washing soda   A product that contains sodium carbonate and can be used to soften permanent hard water

Wegener (Alfred)   The German scientist who proposed the theory of continental drift

Physics glossary

Airbag A safety device in a vehicle that rapidly inflates upon impact. Airbags serve to cushion the driver or passenger from hard objects, e.g. the steering wheel, in a collision

Alpha radiation (α) Radiation that can be stopped by a few centimetres of air or a sheet of paper

Ammeter An instrument for measuring electrical current

Amp (A) The unit of electrical current

Amplitude The maximum height of a wave

Audible hearing range The range of frequencies that humans can hear (20 Hz to 20 kHz)

Average speed The average speed that a vehicle is travelling at over a set distance

Background radiation Radiation that is always around us

Balanced forces Forces that are equal in size and opposite in direction

Battery Two or more electrical cells

Beta radiation (β) Radiation that can be stopped by a few metres of air or a thin sheet of aluminium

Big Bang theory The theory explaining the origin of the Universe. The Big Bang proposes that the Universe originated as a tiny point (a singularity) 14 billion years ago, and has continued to expand ever since

Biofuel Fuel produced from (recently) living material

Blue (coloured) wire The neutral wire in a three-pin plug

Boiler The part of a fossil fuel power station that converts water into steam. The boiler converts thermal energy into kinetic energy

Braking distance The distance a vehicle travels after the brakes are activated until reaching a complete stop

Brown (coloured) wire The live wire in a three-pin plug

Circuit diagram A diagram showing the wiring and components in an electrical circuit

Conventional electrical flow The original (but incorrect) idea that electricity flowed from the positive terminal of a cell or battery around the circuit to the negative terminal

Converging (convex) lens A lens that converges (brings closer together) light rays

Cornea The outer transparent covering of the eye. Most refraction of light takes place in the cornea

Crumple zone A region in a vehicle that 'crumples' and collapses slowly upon impact in a collision, so reducing the force that people inside the vehicle are subjected to

Current The amount of electricity flowing in an electrical circuit

Distance–time graph A graph of distance (on the y-axis) against time (on the x-axis)

Diverging (concave) lens A lens that diverges (bends outwards) light rays

Double insulation Appliances are double insulated if they have an outer plastic (insulated) cover and an inner plastic (insulated) cover around the electrical parts

Dynamo A device for making electricity. Dynamos have a rotating magnet surrounded by coils of wire

Echo Reflected sound

Efficiency The efficiency of an appliance or device describes how good it is at transferring energy from one form to a different, and useful, form

Electrical cell A component that supplies electricity

Electrical (National) Grid The system of pylons and cabling that distributes electricity from power stations around the country

Electricity The flow of electrons through a conductor

Electromagnetic spectrum The range of electromagnetic waves in order of increasing wavelength (and decreasing frequency): gamma rays – X-rays – ultraviolet – visible light – infrared – microwaves – radio waves

Electron A subatomic particle in an atom that has a negligible relative mass and a relative charge of –1. Electrons orbit the atom nucleus in zones called shells

Extender A substance that is added to petrol or diesel to reduce the use of fossil fuels, e.g. the alcohol in gasohol

Flash-bang method A method of measuring the speed of sound in air

Fossil fuel   Fuel formed from the remains of plants and animals that have been compressed by layers of rock for millions of years

Frequency   The number of waves passing a particular point in one second

Friction   The force that opposes motion

Fuel cell   A special type of battery that has raw materials added, e.g. methanol, rather than being recharged as in traditional batteries

Fuse   A safety device in electrical plugs or circuits. The fuse will melt and break the circuit if the current is too high

Galaxy   A huge collection of stars

Gamma radiation (γ)   Highly-penetrating electromagnetic radiation that can be stopped by several centimetres of lead

Gasohol   Fuel produced by adding alcohol to petrol

Generator   The part of a power station that makes electricity (similar in principle to a dynamo). The generator converts kinetic energy to electrical energy

Geocentric   The early model of the Solar System, in which it was thought that the Sun and the planets orbited the Earth

Gravity   The force of attraction that exists between objects

Green and yellow (coloured) wire   The earth wire in a three-pin plug

Half-life   The length of time it takes for half of the atoms in a radioactive element to disintegrate (the length of time it takes for the level of radioactivity to fall by half)

Heliocentric   The current model of the Solar System in which the planets (including Earth) orbit the Sun

Hertz (Hz)   The unit of frequency (1 kHz = 1000 Hz)

Instantaneous speed   Speed at a particular moment in time

Ionising radiation   Radiation that causes ionisation. Atoms become ionised if they lose (or gain) electrons and become charged

Kilowatt-hour (kWh)   The amount of electricity used by an appliance that uses 1000 W of power for a one hour period

Law of Conservation of Energy   The law that states that energy cannot be created or destroyed; it can only be transformed from one form to another

Lens   The part of the eye that focuses light on the retina

Light year   The distance light travels in one year

Long sight   The eye defect in which distant objects can be clearly seen but close-up objects (objects at normal reading distance) are blurred

Longitudinal wave   A wave in which the particles vibrate in the same direction (parallel to) as the direction of travel, e.g. sound

Mobile phone cell   The area serviced by a particular mast

Momentum   The mass of an object multiplied by its velocity (units of momentum are kg m/s)

Neutron   A subatomic particle in an atom's nucleus that has a relative mass of 1 and a relative charge of 0

Newton (N)   The unit of force, e.g. friction

Non-renewable (finite) energy source   A source that will run out because it cannot be replaced

Ohm (Ω)   The unit of resistance

Parallel circuit   A parallel circuit has more than one branch through which electricity can flow

Proton   A subatomic particle in an atom's nucleus that has a relative mass of 1 and a relative charge of +1

Radiation   Radiation is emitted by radioactive elements as their nuclei disintegrate

Radioactive element   An element that has atoms with unstable nuclei due to unstable combinations of protons and neutrons

Reaction time   The time it takes to react to a situation

Red-shift   The phenomenon of the light spectrum of distant galaxies being shifted towards the red end of the spectrum

Refraction   The bending of light rays by a lens

Regenerative braking system   A system in which kinetic energy from braking is converted to electricity by generators linked to vehicle wheels

Regenerative hybrid system   The use of kinetic energy from engine parts to recharge the vehicle battery

Renewable energy   Energy from renewable sources, e.g. hydroelectric power or wind turbines

Residual circuit breaker   A modern electrical safety device that can rapidly stop the flow of current if there is a fault

Resistance   Resistance opposes the flow of electrical current

Resistor   A device that can limit or change the size of electrical current

Resultant force   The force produced as a consequence of unbalanced forces. A resultant force will have both a value and a direction

Retina   The layer at the back of the eye that contains the light-sensitive cells

Rigid passenger cell   The strong rigid cabin that encloses the driver and passengers in a vehicle. It will normally remain intact in a collision preventing those inside from being crushed

Series circuit   A circuit in which the components are connected side by side (in a row)

Short sight   The eye defect in which close-up objects (at normal reading distance) can be clearly seen but distant objects are blurred

Solar System   The Sun and the structures (e.g. planets, comets and asteroids) that orbit it

Speed   How fast an object is travelling. Speed can be measured in metres per second (m/s), kilometres per hour (km/hr) or miles per hour (mph)

Speed bump   A deliberately placed ridge in the road that serves to reduce vehicle speed

Speed limit   The maximum legal vehicle speed in a particular area

Star   A massive extra-terrestrial structure that emits light and radiation

Steady State Theory   An alternative theory (largely discarded) to the Big Bang Theory for the origin of the Universe

Step-down transformer   A device that decreases electrical voltage as electricity leaves the electrical grid and is used by business and homes

Step-up transformer   A device that increases voltage and deceases the current of electricity before it flows through the electrical grid

Stopping distance   The distance travelled between starting to think about stopping and reaching a complete stop

Substitute fuel   Fuel that can be used instead of petrol or diesel, e.g. biofuel

Thinking distance   The distance a vehicle travels while the driver is thinking about what to do

Traffic calming measure   A strategy that helps reduce vehicle speed in a particular area, e.g. road narrowing schemes

Transverse wave   A wave in which the particles vibrate at right angles to the direction of wave travel, e.g. light

Turbine   The part of a power station that drives the generator. A turbine converts kinetic energy (of the turbine) into kinetic energy (in the generator)

Ultrasound   Frequencies higher than 20 kHz

'Unit' of electricity   An 'amount' of electricity that is used when calculating electricity bills

Universe   The space occupied by all the galaxies that exist

Variable resistor (rheostat)   A device that can change the current flowing through a component, e.g. a dimmer light switch

Velocity   The displacement (distance away from starting position) over time

Volt (V) The unit of voltage

Voltage   The amount of electricity supplied to an electrical circuit

Voltmeter   An instrument for measuring voltage

Watts (W) [or kilowatts (kW)]   The units of power

Wavelength   The distance between two successive wave crests or troughs

Weight   The force of gravity on an object is its weight

Index